BIMAL ROY'S

MADHUMATI

BIMAL ROY'S

MADHUMATI

UNTOLD STORIES
FROM BEHIND
THE SCENES

Rinki Roy Bhattacharya

RUPA

Published by
Rupa Publications India Pvt. Ltd 2014
7/16, Ansari Road, Daryaganj
New Delhi 110002

Sales centres:
Allahabad Bengaluru Chennai
Hyderabad Jaipur Kathmandu
Kolkata Mumbai

ISBN:

First impression 2014

10 9 8 7 6 5 4 3 2 1

Typeset in Adobe Jenson Pro by SÜRYA, New Delhi
Printed by Parksons Graphics Pvt. Ltd, Mumbai

Contents

Foreword
Memories of Madhumati

The Indian film industry considers it a matter of pride to claim the distinguished producer/director Bimal Roy—Bimalda, as he was affectionately called—amongst its own fraternity. For me, personally, working with a gifted director like Bimalda was joy doublefold. Not only did he cast me to play Chandramukhi in *Devdas*, but he also reiterated his faith in me with the author-backed role of Madhumati.

Madhumati, the innocent tribal girl from the hills, who burst into song and danced with abandon, was conceived as a mixture of the earthy and the ethereal. Being a dedicated and hard-working director, Bimalda was able to infuse me with his vision of the character and extract the best out of me. He would create a comfortable relationship with his actors effortlessly before gently explaining what he required from us. Thanks to him, every shot of mine was replete with a rich variety of emotions, especially the climax with its dramatic flashbacks wherein I portray the spirit of Madhumati, leaving the audience completely bewitched.

The reincarnation story of *Madhumati* was treated so artistically by Bimalda that it never went beyond the realm of realism he was renowned for. He created a classic par excellent.

The film remains extraordinary in terms of performances, music score, lyrics, cinematography and art direction with picturesque outdoor landscapes adding to its perennial charm.

Bimalda's *Madhumati* will always remain one of the most memorable films of my filmy career. Even today, audiences are mesmerized by this extraordinary film. Working with Bimalda was a great opportunity, a wonderful experience for me.

I am happy that Rinki has penned a detailed account and rekindled memories of her father Bimal Roy, the maker of *Madhumati*.

Dr Vyjayanthimala Bali

Preface
The Book of Memories

The absence of any serious writing on the cinema of renowned auteur Bimal Roy, considered India's foremost neo-realist guru, was a frustrating discovery for me, to be honest. I felt something was broken, a link, a promise. Without a thought about what this involved, singlehandedly, I embarked on a journey to address that unfortunate cultural gap. The fact that Bimal Roy was my father however proved challenging to me as a writer. I experienced a constant struggle to separate the two distinct and powerful identities, the film-maker from my father. For it was important I keep the two apart. If I had to comment dispassionately on the formidable body of his work, I required a distance. In the end, from 1984/5 until 2009, I edited four titles on my film-maker father, Bimal Roy, excluding this book and I am happy to admit, the work turned out to be liberating.

Many of my father's celebrated works, for example, *Do Bigha Zamin*, *Sujata* and *Bandini*, I think, deserve scholarly studies, deserve to be revalued. Why then did I select *Madhumati*, his most uncharacteristic work? It was the result of a fortuitous coincidence that made me select *Madhumati*.

The idea of the book occurred when I was planning a Golden Jubilee celebration of the film. It was important to reconnect with the film's technicians, its stars, and make the occasion authentic and memorable. The Golden Jubilee occasion, intended to be a celebration of an outstanding film, inspired me to explore behind the scenes and find untold stories about the making of *Madhumati*. Meeting individuals involved in the creation of the 1957/8 film was in itself a breakthrough. That, in short, was the start of a pilgrimage into the blurry past with memories echoing all the way.

Before long, I was sitting on a pile of rare, intriguing material about *Bimal Roy's Madhumati*. While different voices spoke to me, a book of memories gently stirred into life. What began as an idle curiosity, a personal query, eventually turned into a pilgrimage. It was difficult to eschew sentimentality in a pilgrimage that uncovered the footprints of my missing father. Apart from nostalgia, the book overflows with rich memories and nuggets of information that holds a mirror to an entirely invisible world. Following these untold stories is an enigmatic film made sixty years ago, and its lasting cinematic legacy is now ready to be read, and told.

As I honour and applaud the memories of forgotten artistes, I also pay homage to my film-maker father, Bimal Roy.

Introduction

I was almost fifteen in 1957 when my father was making *Madhumati*. Regretfully, I remember very little about the making of the film. Actually my memory is equally faint about the making of his other films too. We were kept at a distance from the world of film-making; our household having very little pretensions to the film industry traditions of the period. Stars working with Baba did not visit our home; drink parties never interrupted the even tenor of our rather middle class Bengali household. Even something as innocuous as the popular movie magazine *Filmfare* never crossed our threshold. Growing up in such an austere environment, we were oblivious for the most part about Baba's glamorous profession. It was like living out the title of my favourite Tagore novel, *Ghare-Baire* (*Home and the World*). The two travelled in distinct orbits that never intersected; and oddly, I was devoid of any curiosity to uncover this hidden world of glamour or steal a key to open the studio doors into the heady green rooms from where women emerged as shining stars.

My interest in cinema blossomed only a few years later, when as a student at Elphinstone College, I invited the renowned film scholar Marie Seton[1] to speak on World Cinema. She ended up converting the entire audience that evening; and from passive spectators we all became passionate film watchers. I was inspired enough to join the Anandam Film Society as a life member that very week, with no regrets whatsoever.

On the rare occasion when family and friends trooped to Mohan Studios to watch Baba shoot, I was always surprised by the tedious and tiresome business of film-making. It seemed terribly repetitive, in fact unromantic. The voice that yelled 'Cut!' every few seconds successfully drove away any budding romance from blossoming into an intimate love scene. Another word that startled us was the stern 'Silence'. Film and family life were truly world apart! No wonder my memories of Baba making his films are insignificant, merging with the blurry backdrop against which we were raised.

And therefore, writing about *Madhumati* is a formidable challenge. As a cinematic piece the film is an iconic classic. It stirs deep nostalgic sentiments among those who know it well. I sincerely hope to do justice to its heritage status. Piecing together the threads of its film-making history called for the retracing of a journey that I had never made with Baba. All the anecdotes that have been woven together are recollections from a fast-vanishing era; and what compelled me to overcome the challenges of self-doubt to undertake a fresh, physical journey was that I considered it a story worth documenting.

A couple of incidents brim to the surface and seem promising anecdotes to begin the story. It was around 8.30 pm that night when Baba returned home from the studios in his green and white Chevrolet station wagon. As usual, he changed from the black flannel trousers and white shirt that he wore to work into the fresh white cotton lungi set laid out neatly by George (or whoever was the houseboy). Normally Baba would curl up on the sofa, tucking his long legs under him, and scan *The Times of India* or pick up a Bengali novel from where he had left off. Next would be the familiar orders: '*George, khana laga do!*' followed by his call for us to assemble for dinner. Our dining room was a separate cottage to the rear of the main house; close to the large, primitive and poorly-lit kitchen. I was never able to fathom how sumptuous food was produced without major accidents to the food or the cook.

Our dinner was magnificent as usual, cooked by Alfred, a shy, Mangalorean cook. It was after the meal that I sensed a strange sort of flurry; unusual for our staid Bengali household where dinner heralded the day's concluding chapter. We were summarily sent to bed and obey we did, in that era of unconditional surrender to parental authority. My hushed queries to the ayah and George elicited the information that Sahab had a meeting later that night. Guests were expected; though no one had the faintest idea who they were. Unknown to me, it was to become a night to remember.

My curiosity rose to fever pitch. Late-night meetings at our home were unheard of. Meetings took place in the studio. I roped in my friend Mehroo, our Parsee landlady's imaginative daughter, to lay down plans to investigate. This was too tempting a mystery to miss. Our plan was simple: stay awake and watch. Mehroo came slinking down the banister to join me and the two of us retreated into the shadows of my bedroom, pretending to sleep. Much later in life, it would be the same bedroom where Kersi Katrak (her brother) would join us to finalize my elopement plans with Basu in hushed, frightened tones.

On that night as a gentle drizzle fell, we huddled against the massive teak shuttered-doors, primed for eavesdropping. The guests trooped in; to our disappointment they were no exotic strangers! We knew them all. There was Baba's editor Hrishikesh Mukherjee, Nabendu Ghosh, and dialogue writer Rajinder Singh Bedi, among others. Our intense anticipation was dashed. They settled down in our spacious living room, and soon we heard a voice reading out aloud. Sorely disappointed, we were on the verge of calling off the nocturnal investigation when a car screeched to a halt, crunching the wet gravel. The portico was suddenly alive. Someone had arrived later than the rest! Who could it be? We decided to stay put.

The object of our curiosity had now entered the hall. Clad in pristine white trousers, the shirt formally tucked in, his face was above our eye level. Something familiar in his measured gait niggled at my brain when his profile swung into view. I've never been athletic but at that point I could have easily performed a perfect somersault! Beside me, Mehroo stifled a scream, drawing her breath in time. Clutching each other's hands, we stood rooted to the spot. One more peek was necessary to confirm the unbelievable. Could it really be Dilip Kumar—the one and only heart-throb of all the girls in the world? I pinched myself, and blinked a thousand times. I would swoon I knew, and fall down with a terrific crash bringing the whole household, especially Ma to investigate.

I have to confess a closely-guarded secret at this point! I used to have a picture of Dilip Kumar as Devdas concealed behind my bedroom door. It was the last thing I saw before I went to bed every day; the first when I woke up. I dreamed and prayed fervently to be his beloved. BMW 2424, the number of his light-blue Impala Studebaker, was etched on my heart! Madly in love with the off-screen Yusuf-bhai with all my heart, my head knew that I had to make do with the Devdas picture, his hair brush or his Studebaker car. And there he was, my hero, outside my room!

We listened intently. Yusuf-bhai was the only person who did not sit down; he paced the length of the living room, taut, restless, stopping only to offer incredible suggestions: '*Bimalda, yahan billi ki awaaz honi chahiye...*' (Bimalda, a cat should meow at this point.)

Turning his mouth into a microphone, Yusuf-bhai meowed realistically. I do not know if his suggestions were included in the final script, but I have no doubt that I was witness to a *Madhumati* script session on the single occasion that it was held at home. It thrills me to go back in time to that innocent age when romance quivered within touch, fired by a young girl's unsteady steps towards ecstatic love.

I met an old pen pal Zainab in London, recently, after nearly fifty years. She reminded me: 'Remember, you took us to watch the shooting of your father's film *Madhumati*... We were so excited to see Dilip Kumar. Oooh, how handsome he was!'

Embarrassed to admit that I had no memory of that particular visit to Mohan Studios, I merely nodded. However, I do remember going to the Wilson Dam near Igatpuri along with the film unit. A convoy of cars and vans left early for the location on the long Western Ghat. I did not know that the unit was to shoot the Lata Mangeshkar-solo, *Ghadi ghadi mora dil dhadke*, with the stunning Vyjayanthimala, *Madhumati's* heroine, dancing down the hill. She had travelled regally in her own sedan car with a personal entourage. The pure vegetarian food she favoured came from home as usual. Two huge pieces of wood, akin to pine tree trunks, protruded from a delivery van behind us. When we reached the location, four men carried the trunks to plant them firmly on the hillside while a spot boy ran around sticking artificial crepe flowers here and there. The significance of the artificial pine trunks and fake flowers dawned on me much later. The slopes of Igatpuri had been made to replicate the Kumaon Hills for the song-sequence. On a black and white screen, aided by a clever camera angle, Igatpuri would match Kumaon, the viewers, none the wiser.

Baba's *Madhumati* is worlds away from his other celebrated works like *Do Bigha Zamin* (1953), *Sujata* (1959) or *Bandini* (1963). The film was not inspired by a published Bangla literary work that Baba devoured with great interest. On the contrary, once made, the film created a genre by itself, a template for on-screen ghost stories. *Madhumati*, Baba's ninth work, was an independent film script. It was written specifically as a screenplay for Bimal Roy Productions by his close associate, the maverick director Ritwick Kumar Ghatak[2].

Why did I choose to trace and write the *Madhumati* story and not *Sujata* or *Bandini*? To be honest, I have no simple answer to that. It could have been an intimate personal query, seeking roots to Baba's story-telling heritage. An avid reader, Baba was not a bedside story-teller like many fathers I know. He was the man who spoke in pictures, as the title to the Bimal Roy anthology suggests. Through his wide exposure to World Cinema, his travels abroad, Baba realized the limits of the spoken word. His stories were intended to travel beyond the narrow confines of domestic thresholds, out into the wide world, perhaps even beyond that. His granddaughter Anwesha Arya[3] reminded[4] us: 'Before crossover cinema was considered a genre, Bimal Roy was making cinema cross over, beyond and between borders. His ability to permeate the parameters of language using the universality of film language sets him apart from other film-makers of the period spanning pre-independence and young India.'

It is possible, my partiality to the genre of the ghost story led me to *Madhumati*. But I know that it is an incomplete answer. Having written the book, perhaps I too shall find the answer some day!

I remember the exact moment when I began to think seriously about writing a book on *Madhumati*. I had gone to meet the famous screen villain Pran at his Pali Hill residence with a personal invitation to attend the golden jubilee celebration of *Madhumati* at the local Globus Theatre. People still remember the actor for portraying several villainous parts including that of the *Madhumati* villain, Ugranarayan. Where was that ruthless, swashbuckling bad man of yesteryears who inspired fear in viewers? Before me was a feeble eighty-nine year old man, supported by helpers, looking at the world with a vacant stare.

I experienced a stab of loss bordering on bereavement—confronted by the possibility of losing film history of archival worth. The thespian, on whom a belated Dadasaheb Phalke Award was conferred in 2013, alongwith many others like him, are part of our popular film culture and heritage. He immortalized a large number of pathbreaking films, including *Madhumati*, *Don* (1978), *Amar Akbar Antony* (1977) and *Upkar* (1967) with his performances. Pran's memories were of great value if I wished to document the story. Suddenly, I had an overwhelming desire to know more about the film from those very individuals who created it. But the ravages of age had put their memory at grave risk. I returned from Pran's home, a sadder woman, immersed in uneasy thought. It was that night, on that dark, gloomy night, that *Madhumati*[5] reclaimed me.

And now an extraordinary journey is before me! In three days Maithili and I leave for Ranikhet via Delhi and Kathgodam, in search of people and places, and placing names with faces from the past. I am unsure of what awaits us at the other end or what I will recapture. The very prospect of visiting *Madhumati's* birth place in a misty hill station, a distant dream once, is a thrilling prospect in itself.

NOTES

[1]Marie Seton (20 March 1910–17 February 1985) was an actress, art, theatre and film critic and biographer of Sergei Eisenstein, Paul Robeson, Jawaharlal Nehru and Satyajit Ray. At her request she was cremated, and the plaque of her ashes in Golders Green Crematorium reads: 'Marie Seton Hesson, Padma Bhushan, Citizen of the World'.

[2]Ritwick Kumar Ghatak's cinema is primarily remembered for its meticulous depiction of social reality along with Satyajit Ray and Mrinal Sen. Although their roles were often adversarial, they were ardent admirers of each other's work, and in doing so, the three directors

charted the independent trajectory of parallel cinema, as a counterpoint to the mainstream fare of Hindi cinema in India. Ghatak received quite a few awards in his career, including National Film Awards' Rajat Kamal for Best Story in 1974 for his film *Jukti Takko Aar Gappo*, Best Director's Award from Bangladesh Cine Journalists Association for *Titash Ekti Nadir Naam*. The Government of India honoured him with the Padma Shri for Arts in 1970. Ghatak's first commercial release was *Ajantrik* (1958), a comedy-drama film with a science fiction theme. It was one of the earliest Indian films to portray an inanimate object, in this case an automobile, as a character in the story. Ghatak's greatest commercial success as a script writer was *Madhumati* (1958), one of the earliest films to deal with the theme of reincarnation. It was a Hindi film directed by film-maker Bimal Roy whose assistant he had been. The film earned Ghatak his first award nomination, for the Filmfare Best Story Award. Ritwick Ghatak directed eight full-length films. Ghatak's only major commercial success was *Madhumati* (1958), a Hindi film for which he wrote the screenplay.

[3]See list of contributors.

[4]For further reading, read Anwesha Arya's essay: 'Beyond Borders: Bimal Roy at Home and Abroad' from *Bimal Roy—The Man Who Spoke in Pictures*, Editor Rinki Roy Bhattacharya.

[5]*Madhumati* was launched in front of the Karlovy Vary International Film Festival Theatre in Czechoslovakia. Dilip Kumar faced the camera, while Soviet actress Tatjana Konjuchova, switched on the camera. Polish actress Barbara Polonska acted as clapper loader. *Madhumati* is the first Indian film to be launched abroad.

I

Untold Stories

1

The Beginning

*This interplay of light and dark constitutes life, although in the
world of movies, there are times when the dividing lines between
them cease to exist.*

—Saadat Hasan Manto

The journey to Ranikhet was nowhere on my agenda, nor was
this book when Taran Khan[1], a bright, young journalist came to
interview me about Bombay Talkies[2] (BT), the erstwhile studio
where Baba directed *Maa* (1952), his first film in Bombay. I had
no inkling that meeting her would open the doors to the
Madhumati location story; that her aunt, Razia Husain[3], held
the keys to several secret chambers.

Everything happened swiftly, as if scripted by a clever writer.
We were chatting about films and journalism after Taran had
completed the interview, when I casually mentioned that I may
consider a book project on *Madhumati*. She sat up in her chair:
'*Madhumati*? Oh that is our family favourite. We have watched
the film many times.'

'Why is it such a family favourite?' I asked, as if destiny was
leading me on.

'It is quite a story,' Taran smiled, mysteriously. 'My aunt

caused a huge scandal when she ran out of the house without wearing a dupatta after she heard that Dilip Kumar was shooting in the vicinity of her grandfather's estate for *Madhumati*! Her most prized possession even today is a snapshot with Dilip Kumar taken during the outdoor shooting of the film in Ghorakhal.'

It was my turn to sit up. This young woman who I had met by sheer accident was claiming that her aunt had actually witnessed the outdoor shooting of *Madhumati*! Unbelievable, simply unbelievable! Trying hard to maintain my composure, I quizzed Taran: 'Where is Ghorakhal? I have never heard that name before. And I know for sure that the *Madhumati* outdoor was shot in Nainital.'

'But I have grown up hearing stories about *Madhumati* being shot in Ghorakhal and how Dilip Kumar had lunch with the family. My aunt remembers it all. She would be happy to give you all the details. You should call her.'

Though excited beyond measure, I retained enough composure to request Taran to warn the lady in question that I would be contacting her soon.

Bhowali, Ghorakhal, Gethia, Rampur! These names began to dance luminously before my eyes. Places that I had never heard of nor knew existed on the map. Our belief that *Madhumati* was shot in Nainital or Ranikhet began to crumble under the weight of emerging evidence. Taran's visit had truly been a revelation, a breakthrough; it was *the* missing link that I had been waiting for to start my story—my pilgrimage into the blurry past.

I decided to call Taran's aunt Razia, the lady who caused local flutter fifty years ago by running out without a dupatta, later that night. I simply had to hear it straight from her. Throwing caution to the wind, I made a late night call to Razia. She was naturally surprised and overwhelmed to be talking to Bimal Roy's daughter. In a voice soaked with nostalgia, Razia mused: '*Kitni baatein yaad aati hain, tasveer si ban jati hai*! That afternoon when I heard Dilip Kumar was shooting in the neighbourhood, I insisted trudging down all the way to Bhowali where the unit was lodged in a guest house. But alas! Nobody was to be found there!'

I made Razia promise that she would email every detail she could recall about the *Madhumati* shooting, especially about meeting her heart-throb—and of course mine too—Dilip Kumar. I put down the phone reluctantly that night, full of regret that Aligarh was too far away to dash down for a hearty chat with Razia in between sips of chai. One thing was certain—Razia and Taran had sounded the clapper...all that was required now was the clarion call of 'Action' for me to start rolling.

The other thought that occupied me was how I could re-trace the footsteps of the production house which created that film—Bimal Roy Productions or BRP[4] for short. The BRP story was significant, especially now that the production house is virtually extinct, except as a credit by-line in Baba's film titles with the Rajabai Tower image of the Bombay University logo, chiming before the start of a BRP film. BRP and *Madhumati* are therefore, inexorably linked.

Bombay Talkies was relatively fortunate in this respect. Film Historian Amrit Ganger was commissioned to write 'Franz Osten and the Bombay Talkies: Journey from Munich to Malad' (Max Mueller Bhavan, Bombay, 2001). Another slice of good luck for the studios lay in the virtue of having Saadat Hasan Manto as part of the Bombay Talkies writing department. A large slice of that period was saved for posterity. The brilliant Urdu storyteller was a practicing journalist as well and his racy snapshots of Bombay Talkies and spicy profiles of the 1940s stars are sparkling gems to read in the collection titled *Stars from Another Sky*. I strongly recommend this book to anyone interested in that bygone era. It is heartening that young writers like Taran are still filing stories on Himanshu Rai and the Bombay Talkies era, striving to retain them in the stream of consciousness, albeit briefly. Other institutions, dating to the same period, had slim chances and remain largely undocumented. India's track record of archiving film history is hopelessly inadequate to its gargantuan film production. Notwithstanding a handful of private collectors, the public has forgotten early film history.

Razia was holidaying in Ladakh those days. My eagerness to hear her story had to be put on hold. I concentrated on the other project, the BRP story, garnering anecdotes and titbits from some of its leading star cast, some celebrated, some lesser mortals—all equally authentic; bringing back memories and voices from the distant past to paint the larger picture Bimal Roy Productions, it seems, was conceived on a ride in a running BEST bus. This extraordinary piece of information sounds both absurd and appropriate. It stands to reason that a production house that specialized in films addressing pertinent social issues relevant to young India should have such a public birth place, the common bus. The fact that a famous film director travelled in a public transport and watched films with the public, speaks of an era of relative safety. But those days, the underworld was unborn. The filmdom faced no imminent threat from its dark denizians. Such a situation is inconceivable these days when, directors, stars—and of course politicians—live cloistered lives with half a dozen beefy gun-toting men protecting them at all times.

Accepting the fact that I knew Bimal Roy only as a daughter knows her father, I began to assiduously gather information about him. Several years had gone by since Baba had passed away. And some of his important colleagues had joined him by the time I began my restless quest. It was about the same period that the Madhya Pradesh Film Development Corporation (MPFDC) entrusted me with the writing of a book on Bimal Roy. I did not have the heart to warn them that I lacked the confidence to handle the enormous responsibility of writing about Bimal Roy. Curiously, though the disadvantage made me nervous, it also succeeded in motivating me. And so a scrappy book was produced, to be promptly disowned by me.

But it served a purpose. In that state of mind, as the thirsty roams in search of water, I visited Baba's colleagues, one by one in the hope of educating myself about my enigmatic father. Naïvely, I believed that Baba's technical crew, acquainted with his working life, would remember vital details. I realized it was about time that Baba's professional life was documented. This important task seemed to have been laid aside; I was therefore honour-bound to unearth the film-maker in my father.

The first person I went to meet was Hrishikesh Mukherjee[5] whom we knew as Hrishikaka. Before he went on to become a famous director himself, he had edited all of Baba's major films including *Madhumati*. Working intimately during the film-making process, directors and editors tend to behave like a married couple. I had witnessed Hrishikaka interact with Baba, freely without fear or intimidation. Unlike Baba's other assistants, he possessed a unique ability to get around people, including the sphinx-like Bimal Roy. This worked in Hrishikaka's favour. A charismatic man, he was voluble, wrote and recited limericks at the drop of a pin, cracked us up with jokes and mimicry—all this making him an instant favourite. Confident that he possessed rare nuggets about their relationship and knew stories about his silent, reticent director, I found myself at Hrishikaka's Carter Road home one evening. And the entertainer par excellence lived up to his reputation. He regaled me with the recent limericks he had written, including an unflattering one on me. He gave huge headlines to his terrible health conditions, his painful gout. I managed to grab a minute when he paused to gently veer the conversation towards Baba, which was the main focus of my visit. A cold monsoon wind swept past making the glass window panes shudder in anticipation.

'Hrishikaka', I began tentatively, 'How was it working with Baba? Was he always quiet? How did he explain scenes to his actors if he did not talk? How did he direct?'

The effect of my question was unexpected, infact, it was dramatic. Hrishikaka, who had been chattering non-stop, stopped as if struck. So dramatic was the change in him, that for a moment, I was afraid something was wrong, that he had taken ill. Assuring myself that he was fine, I repeated the question. He looked away, absently stroking the black dog resting at his feet. I was about to ask once again when I heard him say to no-one in particular: 'There are two individuals I never talk about—Dadamoni (Ashok Kumar) and Bimalda. Never ask me about them.'

His lapse into sulky silence seemed to call the evening to a close and presuming that I had offended him, I got up to leave when he perked up: 'Khuku (my pet name), do you know how Bimal Roy Productions was born?'

Without giving me a chance to reply he went on:

> 'Then listen. We were returning to Malad in a double-decker bus one night after watching Akira Kurosawa's *Rashomon*[6] at the Eros cinema. All of us were lost in our thoughts; the film had made a tremendous impact on us. I remember asking Bimalda why we couldn't make films like *Rashomon*. He sunk into a reverie before exclaiming: "Who will write the film?"
>
> "*Keno, ami likhbo* (Why, I shall write)," I replied at once.
>
> We decided that all the unit members would have an equal share in the production company and that is how Bimal Roy Productions was born, on a BEST bus!'

At the end of this incredible story he grinned wickedly, much like the proverbial Cheshire cat. I realized that Hrishikaka had amply compensated his stubborn refusal to talk about Baba by narrating that single anecdote. It was a telling tale of easy camaraderie, trust, commitment and conviction. It was evocative of the fine equation between Baba and his band. These, as I discovered by and by, were the common norms and ideals of the post-independence work culture, especially in the Bimal Roy Productions.

BRINGING THEM INTO FOCUS

Bimal Roy Productions could not have had a better introduction than Hrishikaka's tale. The 'we' Hrishikaka mentioned so casually were his other BRP colleagues—the comedian Asit Sen (who doubled as Baba's chief assistant for many years) and script writer Nabendu Ghose[7]. They had shifted base from Kolkata to Mumbai with Baba in the first phase of our migration. The second phase brought art director Sudhendu Roy, character actor Nazir Hussain, and cameraman Kamal Bose. The last to join was composer Salil Chowdhury, Bengal's gift to the world of Indian music. Nabendu Ghose speaks eloquently of Bimal Roy and the men who surrounded him, in his keynote paper 'My Film Guru', with the following remarks and I quote him:

> 'An outstanding contribution of Bimal Roy to the Indian Cinema are his many disciples, all names to contend with. They are the editor-director Hrishikesh Mukherjee, Asit Sen, Moni Bhattacharya, Ritwik Ghatak, Basu Bhattacharya, Manik Chatterjee, the composer Salil Chowdhury, art director Sudhendu Roy and the lyricist Gulzar. These men have risen to eminence in their chosen fields and made films that bear the stamp of humanism. That I believe is the true hallmark of an institution.'

Hrishikesh Mukherjee was the most successful of all his BRP colleagues. Impatient to strike out on his own, his debut film *Musafir* (1957) went to floors simultaneously with *Madhumati*. This upset the apple cart since he was the official BRP editor.

Elsewhere in this book, veteran editor Dasbabu and Sakharam Borsay, the assistant editor, give their accounts of that troubled time in BRP. Incidentally, *Madhumati* was Hrishikaka's last film for Bimal Roy Productions.

There were two Asit Sens in the Hindi film industry giving rise to many misconceptions. Come to think of it, there were two Bimal Roys working in Bombay; also giving rise to great confusion! The other Bimal Roy was an editor by profession. I have been asked whether Baba edited a particular film, where the other Bimal Roy's name appears as editor in the credits. In this chapter I refer to Asit Sen, the popular and plump comedian of several films. He directed two films, *Parivar* (1956) and *Apradhi Kaun* (1957) for the BRP. Composer Salil Chowdhury tried his hand at direction, albeit unsuccessfully, for an outside production house. Titled *Pinjre Ke Panchhi* (1966), it starred Meena Kumari, my favourite Hindi actress, in the female lead. How ironic that Meenaji left her renowned husband Kamal Amrohi during the making of this film with a telltale name—the caged bird. Many fingers were pointed at Salil Chowdhury and Gulzar after that episode of Meenaji's leaving Kamal Amrohi. Before she took the bold step, Meena Kumari endured great personal and economic hardship for several years; and the most tragic fall out was her lonely death in penury. Her death, however, proved to be a boon for her swan song *Pakeezah* (1972). It was the diva's farewell to the industry where she had lived in a gilded cage. The film took fourteen years to reach the silver screen and was declared a flop when it was released weeks before she passed away on 31 March 1972. But in her death, Meena Kumari (Mahjabeen Bano) immortalized *Pakeezah*.

How ironic and unjust life can be!

When Baba was making *Parineeta* (1953) at Bombay Talkies, I would watch the fragile and slim Meena Kumari, secretly worshipping her beauty and charm. She was pining for her

Kamal Sahab at that time. I believe he used to visit Baba's set on some pretext dressed impeccably in a dark sherwani suit. In yet another corner of the studios, a romance was brewing more cautiously between her sister Mumtaz and Mehmood, whose career as a comedian was yet to take off. I wonder if their singer son, Lucky Ali has heard of his parents' romantic interlude; perhaps he could compose a sentimental ditty for them.

According to Debu Sen, my main informant, Gulzar's cousin brother owned at least four car garages in the suburbs of Bombay. The cousin would sternly summon the errant poet to join their lucrative family business but to no avail. The future lyricist's heart was naturally not in tune with the unromantic world of tinkering nuts and bolts; he simply wished to be left alone to soak in the creative ambience of BRP and hang out with Debu and my husband Basu. For a while Gulzar (according to Debu) did languish as an obscure mechanic, painting cars in the heart of Bombay's red light area. But the lyrics of *Bandini* (1963) ended his struggles and poetic justice triumphed. Sachin Dev Burman's immortal composition and Lataji's divine rendition of *Mora gora ang leyile* stamped Gulzar as a lyricist to reckon with. The rest is history.

Madhumati's commercial success changed tracks for a few of its technicians too. Soon after the film, Baba entrusted Moni Bhattacharjee[8], his production controller, with the direction of *Usne Kaha Tha* (1960) for BRP. The film was also the start of a fruitful relationship between Moni Bhattacharjee and the film's hero, Sunil Dutt. Soon Dutt's production house assigned Bhattacharjee to direct what was to be his best known work, the black and white dacoit saga *Mujhe Jeene Do* (1963).

Raghunath Jhalani and Debabrata Sen were the two chief assistant directors in the *Madhumati* unit. Jhalani possessed a first-class Master's degree in Hindi from Delhi University. In an industry saturated with hypocrisy, exploding with illiterates and parvenus, I doubt if his distinction of holding a degree was perceived as an asset. Of Jhalani's many films, *Anamika* (1973) is easily the best remembered. Amongst Baba's assistant directors—Raghunath Jhalani, Moni Bhattacharjee and Debabrata Sen—Debu, the last survivor from the BRP era, is my main informant as mentioned and a vital link in relating to memories of BRP days and reinventing details about *Madhumati*.

THE ARCHITECT OF MODERN INDIAN CINEMA

1952—the year it was agreed to float BRP, Baba had already completed *Maa* for Bombay Talkies. But he was uncomfortable with his debut in the Bombay film industry. *Maa's* lukewarm reception made him apprehensive about his future in the glamourous Bombay movie industry. It is well-known that he was ready to go back to West Bengal. He was acknowledged as one of Bengal's leading directors, in fact, the leading director of that period. Being a Bengali at heart, he longed for his roots, for the familiar Kolkata ambience.

Two major events held him back. First, floating BRP, his own production company. And second, a new directorial assignment from actor Ashok Kumar to adapt Saratchandra Chatterjee's charming novel, *Parineeta*. Ashok Kumar and debonair Hiten Chaudhury[9] were the two individuals who engineered Baba's move to Bombay. Since they were major shareholders in Bombay Talkies, Baba could not refuse his benefactor Ashok Kumar's request. *Parineeta* and *Do Bigha Zamin* began to be shot simultaneously in 1953.

Parineeta was shot mainly during day shifts at the Bombay Talkies sound stage with a skeletal staff. *Do Bigha Zamin*—the first Bimal Roy Productions film—was shot at night in Mohan Studios on Kurla Road, Andheri-East. Baba established his production banner in the same studio, occupying a vast area of rented premises. He never owned a studio, incidentally, nor did he aspire to despite having the resources to do so. K. Asif's studio was adjacent to Mohan; Guru Dutt's stood nearby too. Mehboob Studio came up in Bandra where we lived. The character-actor Jayant lived in a dilapidated house opposite Mehboob. His sons, like two wrestlers, Imtiaz and Amjad Khan hung around the Hill Road bus terminus ogling at girls. On our return from school we literally ran up the hill in fright!

Raj Kapoor too had his own studio in Chembur. It is one of the last Bombay movie studios to survive. RK's stylish logo of a man with a violin holding a woman in an intimate embrace never fails to impress me. All of Baba's contemporaries owned studios; but he was content to work in a rented studio, live and die in a rented home. Not owning any private property was his unshaken principle. I remember overhearing an argument between my parents, one of the most loved couples in the film industry. The argument arose when Ma wanted Baba to buy a home. Baba admonished her: 'Property is the cause of human misery. It brings unhappiness.'

Tragically, his words were to be proven right after he passed away. Incidentally Mohan Studios, his workplace, was often mistaken as his property. In fact during his lifetime, Mohan Studios was better known as Bimal Roy Studios.

Baba's mistrust of creating, of amassing private wealth, his open contempt for the feudal class, his mockery of the pompous, rich and powerful recur as a subtext in films like *Udayer Pathe* (1944). It seeped into most of the stories he wrote, the films he made. Through these stories of the elite exploiting the working class, he renounced the feudal class he was born into. His idealistic vision did not permit the excess of wealth or the indulgences it invariably brought. Many speak of Baba as a modern film-maker in this respect. Naseeruddin Shah has commented in his writing that Bimal Roy had a modern approach to story-telling. He asserts: 'The truth is that the acting we consider modern today is the result of a long, tedious process that started long before any of us were born or even thought of, and it was people like Bimal Roy who made that process possible.'

Amongst others who consider Bimal Roy as the architect of modern Indian cinema is Lord Meghnad Desai: 'It is difficult today, fifty and more years since *Pather Panchali*, to realize that *Do Bigha Zamin* was the first modern film that had found a place in post-war world cinema.'

These critics besides many others have put Baba's cinematic contribution in the context of World Cinema. I will leave the reader to decide whether Baba was a modern story-teller or not; my job is to share stories about his larger than life vision, affirming his humanity.

UNSUNG BEHIND THE SCENES

Not everyone attains celebrity status in the quicksand of film-making business. Sadly, many remain unsung. An unremarkable and modest man by appearance, Debabrata Sen, undisputably heads that list among Baba's band of technicians. At eighty-six, he is the sole eyewitness to the BRP era and its forgotten legacy. Debu's memory is fading fast; he punctuates every conversation with the alarming announcement, '*Amar mone nei!*' (I do not remember!) And yet he has dug out innumerable tales, drenched with nostalgia from his faltering memory. As my main informant, Debu has helped me flesh out people from that bygone era. My thirst for BRP anecdotes has found a perfect watering hole in him. And these tales are all he possesses to link him to the Bimal Roy legacy.

Debu vividly recalls the day he had to interview the famous Bimal Roy for a private Bengali monthly, *Prabashi*. Once the interview got over, my father, it seems had remarked: 'People like you must join the film industry.'

Not to be upstaged, Debu quickly replied: 'Why not? I would, if a director like Bimal Roy asked me to work for him.'

Debu brings to life Godiwala Bungalow's vast drawing room: Baba sitting in his home clothes with a cup of tea in one hand and a cigarette in the other, while Debu perched deferentially on one of the ornate Jacobean chairs.

He was rewarded with an appointment for the very next morning. Debabrata Sen went to meet director Bimal Roy at his Mohan Studios office. Sitting in his modest Yaari Road flat, Debu makes a brave effort to recapture incidents, not just about *Madhumati*, but he rewinds to the times. Looking down at his feet, Debu suddenly burst out laughing as if someone had tickled him: 'That day when I went to meet Bimalda at Mohan, you know what? He made me wait the entire day. I understood much later that Bimalda was testing my patience; it was his way of mentoring. And goodness, what patience he had…'

Leaving that thread of memory incomplete, he continued; 'When the title of the film was being exposed, Bimalda said to me: "You need to shorten your name; otherwise it will go out of frame!" From that day Debabrata became Debu; it was at Bimalda's request!'

Debu remembers another personal incident, visibly moved. Once a sister of his was due to be married. Debu was in desperate need of funds. Instead of asking the Bimal Roy Productions cashier Mehta-ji, Debu mustered up the courage to meet the boss directly:

'That particular day Bimalda was sitting alone in his office, reading the Gajendranath Mitra novel *Nari O Niyati*. Even though he saw me, Bimalda continued with his reading. After waiting for a few minutes, I summoned the nerve to tell him that I had a serious matter to discuss with him. Wordlessly, he shut the book and laid it on the table to look at me. I started talking desperately—I needed some money urgently etc. I broke off mid-sentence and silence cloaked the room…

"How much?" he asked suddenly.

"Five thousand. One of my sisters is getting married."

"How many sisters do you have?"

"Seven."

"Which one is this?"

"The youngest."

"Hmm…" He picked up the novel once again.

There was no response to my request; yet I waited hopefully for a long time deciding to leave the room. A lively carrom game was in progress under the big tree opposite his office. I joined in without enthusiasm. Suddenly the BRP office door opened, and the cashier Mehta-ji beckoned to me and handed over a cheque signed by Bimalda for a sum of five thousand rupees. I knew that day that I was not just a Bimal Roy Productions man; I belonged to the entire Bimal Roy joint family.'

BRP'S SPECIAL FEATURES

In between work, especially when there was no shooting, the BRP technicians entertained themselves playing lively games of carrom under the ancient Mango tree. Some played a brisk round of badminton. These were regular recreation features for the Bimal Roy Productions members. Dilip Kumar joined in regularly. Johnny Walker, a carrom master, usually played for the K. Asif team and trounced everyone.

'On the fourth of every month, I received a salary of three hundred rupees,' Debu continued, 'while the senior technicians received five hundred rupees. Do you know the salary was more than sufficient for us in those times. Provident fund contributions and income tax was deducted from our salaries. I must also tell you, Bimal Roy Productions was the only film company to contribute to its workers' provident fund. You must mention this important fact, Rinki.'

Carrom games under the sprawling tree in the studio compound, special film shows in the recording theatres, the annual Mohan Studio Saraswati Puja, where all of us served *prasad* to workers—memories of these simple joys invade the mind. Puja evenings were redolent with incense smoke, fragrant jasmine, and the sounds of the Kathak Queen Sitara Devi's madly dancing anklets as twilight melted into night. On other days, it could be the plaintive notes from Pandit Ram Narain's melodious sarangi that filled the packed puja hall. Baba was partial to some of these stalwarts of Indian classical music. His personal favourites were the sarod maestro Ustad Ali Akbar Khan and the Kathak dancer Sitara Devi.

On the last day of the year, a roaring bonfire at midnight would set aflame all the old calendars bringing the year to its conclusion. These old fashioned recreations BRP unit members enjoyed may appear outdated today, but in those days it was an exhilarating way to unwind. I remember how eagerly Baba would load his small Vauxhall car after an exhausting day at work. All of us at home and his assistants would laughingly struggle for space before setting off on a long drive to the Milk Colony Park blooming with seasonal flowers. We children would spread out on the lush green lawn while the grownups talked in low voices about the next day's shooting or other serious adult talk. The passage time was blissfully forgotten. It was an age of joyous innocence, of wonder and of dreams, many of which were made to come true. Our caring parents made them happen.

Like many of his contemporaries of the Nehruvian age, my father, Bimal Roy, chose to tread the moral high ground. This is apparent from the content of the films he made and the manner in which he negotiated life. Written fifty-nine years ago, poet Shailendra's poignant lyrics from the *Do Bigha Zamin* theme song echo Baba's yearning for immortality, imaging footprints for posterity. That song was his signature tune:

'Dharti kahe pukaar ke,
Beej bichaale pyaar ke,
Mausam beeta jaaye,
Apni kahani chhodd jaa,
Kuch toh nishaani chhod jaa,
Kaun kahe is ore, tu phir aaye na aaye...'[10]

Selecting stories from the BRP album is an unfinished business for the moment—to be continued in later chapters. Razia beckons me with her memories of *Madhumati*. Vacation over, she has sent me her first email which begins on a wistful note: *'Kitni saari baatein yaad aati hain, tasveer si bann gayi hai...'*

Let us move beyond the walls of Mohan Studios, in any case it no longer exists. Swallowed up by real estate builders in the manner of Bombay Talkies, it lies buried under grotesque industrial galas resembling a ghost town.

To Razia who has finally picked up the threads of her *Madhumati* story:

'It was the summer of 1957. I was a starry-eyed girl of about thirteen, just having finished the final examinations of class nine. As our old station wagon heaved up the winding road to Bhowali for our annual summer holiday, the entire brood of nine (or was it eight then?) of various ages and sizes sang all the way up, for we loved the hills. Our destination was Ghorakhal, the summer seat of the Nawab of Rampur. My father was the engineer of Rampur State. We reached Bhowali around noon and were surprised to see a large number of cars blocking the road to Ghorakhal. Unusual, after all there were few motor vehicles in those times. The road leading up to the Estate House lined with pine trees and apple orchards beckoned us. We were filled with excitement as the stately manor loomed ahead.

It was after lunch that the Rampur Estate manager casually remarked about the film shooting nearby. I can still remember my heart performing a somersault when he mentioned Dilip Kumar. Unable to contain myself, I insisted on going down all the way to Bhowali on foot that afternoon, to catch sight of the unit lodged in a guest house. But alas! All of them had gone out for shooting. When I came back tired and dejected, Daddy was sitting in the balcony overlooking the hills smoking his hookah. I related my woes to him; he simply smiled and said "*Tum bekaar gaeen. Woh log toh yahin aayenge.*" And lo and behold, within half an hour, cars started coming up the secluded area of our estate, intent on location hunting. Bimal Roy Sahab and Dilip Sahab sat talking with Daddy on the balcony for a long time. Dusk fell as Dilip Sahib reminisced about an earlier time when he was shooting for *Sangdil* (1952) with Madhubalaji!

To this day I wonder how my father could have predicted their coming—he became my hero for life!

Next day the entire unit descended upon us—cars, vans, cameras et al. Our front lawn was full of people; the quiet Ghorakhal estate had suddenly come to life. Bimalda and Dilip Sahab arrived soon after. Bimalda looked pre-occupied—busy with cameras and shots. And oooh Gawd! Dilip Sahab! Sooo handsome!'

I had not experienced the joy of *Madhumati's* outdoor shooting personally, nor seen trees laden with peach and apple blossoms in spring but the pastoral image sprung to life with Razia's meticulous snapshots. Ghorakhal, Bhowali, Rampur—though names yet, began to dance seductively before my eyes, beckoning to me. I realized that Razia's email was a visa; my motivation to make the journey to these places I never saw nor knew existed. Razia Husain is the only '*chasmadeed gawah*' (a phrase I have grown up hearing onscreen in court-room dramas) who can tell us that story.

We were already into the first week of June. I had to remember to book my train tickets for Kathgodam urgently. The hills were literally alive with the sound of music, beckoning me as a pilgrim...

NOTES

[1]Excerpted from Taran Khan's feature on Bombay Talkies published on 1 July 2012 in the *Hindustan Times*: 'My father came to Bombay at the studio's invitation to make *Maa* in 1950,' recalls Rinki Bhattacharya, daughter of late director Bimal Roy. 'He was paid Rs 15,000—a huge amount at the time—since the management felt that getting good directors could revive their fortunes.' For over two years, her family lived in Devika Rani's bungalow—where her father restored its large garden. There were echoes of past glory—Wirsching shot *Maa*, and Malad still buzzed with creative people linked to the studio. But the closest they got to the spirit of Bombay Talkies was through stories told by old servants, of Himanshu Rai's ghost riding through the compound on a white horse.

[2]A renowned studio founded in 1934, BT folded up by the 1950s. A premiere film-making studio—like New Theaters of Kolkata—Bombay Talkies had on its staff internationally reputed directors like Franz Osten, Niranjan Pal, Himanshu Ray, besides the star Devika Rani and enjoyed global recognition.

[3]See list of contributors.

[4]Abbreviation of Bimal Roy Productions.

[5]Hrishikesh Mukherjee (1922–2006) was a famous Indian film director known for a number of films including *Satyakam*, *Chupke Chupke*, *Anupama*, *Anand*, *Abhimaan*, *Guddi*, *Gol Maal*, *Aashirwad*, *Bawarchi* and *Namak Haraam*. He directed forty-two films during his career spanning over four decades, and is known as the pioneer of the 'middle cinema' of India. He worked with Bimal Roy in Mumbai as film editor and assistant director from 1951, participating in the landmark Roy films *Do Bigha Zamin* and *Devdas*.

[6]*Rashomon* (1950). The renowned Japanese crime drama directed

by Akira Kurosawa. *Rashomon* introduced Kurosawa and the cinema of Japan to western audiences and it is considered one of his masterpieces. The film won the Golden Lion at the Venice Film Festival and also received an Honorary Award at the 24th Academy Awards.

[7]Nabendu Ghosh (1917–2007) was an acclaimed author in Bengali literature. He has written the screenplays of various classic Bollywood movies. Amongst others, he is particularly known for the screenplays of *Sujata, Bandini, Devdas, Majhli Didi, Abhimaan* and *Teesri Kasam*. He has also acted in *Do Bigha Zamin, Teesri Kasam* and *Prahaar*. Later in his career, he directed *Trishagni* (1988).

[8]Moni Bhattacharjee is best known for the dacoit film *Mujhe Jeene Do* (1963), starring Sunil Dutt and Waheeda Rehman. It was shortlisted as an 'Official Selection', for the 1964 Cannes Film Festival. '*Hindu*' a leading newspaper of the time, praised *Mujhe Jeene Do*, with these words 'Brilliant synthesis of script, photography, music, lyrics, acting and direction sends you on an emotional rollercoaster'.

[9]Hiten Chaudhury: The younger brother of economist Sachin Chaudhury (founder of *The Economic Weekly*, now known as the *The Economic & Political Weekly*, in 1949) and the older brother of renowned sculptor Sankho Chaudhury. Hiten Chaudhury was a shareholder in the Bombay Talkies Studios. Along with actor Ashok Kumar, he was a powerful decision-maker at the studios from Devika Rani's time.

[10]The lyrics are from a memorable song in Bimal Roy's *Do Bigha Zamin*, composed by Salil Chowdhury; rendered evocatively by Manna Dey.

2

The Start of a Long Journey

Scriptwriting for a film is the toughest part of the whole racket...the least understood and the least noticed.

—Frank Capra,
Hollywood director

Razia's road map combined with Deep Bhatt's assurances convinced me that the logical step forward would be to visit the actual *Madhumati* location site in Ranikhet before, not after, writing the book. We were already in the first week of June, the summer holidays had commenced; it was going to be extremely difficult to get to the hills. As I was ruminating on these, it struck me that Maithili would be the perfect travelling companion on the *Madhumati* trail. She agreed spontaneously. An ideal travelling companion plus local Ranikhet contacts at the end of the journey were clearly auspicious omens. I arranged for us to take the overnight Kathgodam Express, a train strongly recommended by those who frequent the sector.

An introduction to Deep Bhatt[1], who had sprung out of thin air during the preparatory phase of the book, seems appropriate. It was around March when I received a call from a stranger who introduced himself as Deep Bhatt, a senior reporter from the

Hindustan Times, Nainital. He said he was writing a story about Bimal Roy's contribution to Indian cinema for a language magazine and called me in that connection. The mention of Nainital was enough to get me interested. And so when he called a second time, I could not resist the temptation to ask: 'Deep, I am thinking of writing a book on *Madhumati*. You are from Nainital, perhaps you could find some details about where my father shot the film, where was the production unit stationed? Is it possible for you to ask around for any stories, any leads about that period?'

Though Deep is based in the plains in Haldwani, some distance from Nainital, he was enthusiastic: '*Zaroor, main pooch-taach toh kar hi sakta hoon.*' (Sure, I can at least make inquiries).

Haldwani! A new name added to the growing cluster—Bhowali, Ranikhet, Nainital, Ghorakhal, Gethia and now Haldwani.

Pressing chores had to be accomplished before we took the Ranikhet trip. With monsoon looming ahead, it was imperative for me to visit my Navghar farm.

The narrow road which links the Western Express Highway to Navghar (District Raigarh) had become a metaphor of the *Madhumati* landscape. For the past couple of years, I have come to know the road intimately. You could call it a road to serenity, leading me to a sanctuary, a home away from home. Driving down the forested road, I would often imagine myself transported into the *Madhumati* landscape, unwittingly humming a few strains from the song *Suhana Safar*. Each time I passed, I never ceased to wonder at the sense of déjà vu that swept over me as we entered the luxuriant forest with teak, harda, mahua, palash and khair trees; so different from hill-station flora, yet they never failed to remind me of *Madhumati*.

A SURREAL COINCIDENCE

Imagine my astonishment, when I came across an interview of cinematographer Dilip Gupta, where he talks extensively about shooting *Madhumati* with a detailed account of the film's opening sequence. You could have knocked me down with a feather! The opening sequence was shot within a few kilometres from where I turn into the Khopoli exit on the Western Express Highway! It was a surreal coincidence. I had goosebumps reading his interview. Baba and his cameraman Dilip Gupta had chosen one of the many hair pin bends on the Old Khandala Road to start the eerie narrative. It served to explain the sudden rush of nostalgia that enveloped me when I travelled on the route they had taken more than fifty-five years ago.

Dilip kaka, as I called him, has left a richly detailed account of how he visualized the *Madhumati* opening sequence:

> 'The opening scene of *Madhumati* takes place at night. The shooting was done at night and not in the day. I don't believe in the Day-for-Night technique for the simple reason that it does not give the feeling of real night. We shot the opening scene in the Khandala Ghats. I started shooting at dusk, a little after sunset. In the scene, Dilip Kumar's car is coming through the Ghats. Parts of the road were seen in its headlights. The road was wet because of rain. This gave us a long reflection of the car's headlights. The camera framed the shot in such a way that we had a long area filled with highlight against the dark background. I got the headlights of our car to give some illumination to the coming car. There was no additional lighting. The watchman of the haveli was to come with a lantern in his hand. I put an Inky Dinky bulb in the lantern. It was controlled by a dimmer. The watchman was lit with the lantern and Dilip Kumar and his friend were lit with other studio sources.'[2]

Famous actors, we know, have body doubles, especially for risky scenes. Places too, it seems, have their body doubles. The Tansa Lake, for example, could be used in place of Kashmir's Dal Lake. Film-making, from start to finish, is a game of deception, of make-believe. Humourist George Mikes[3] wrote that wealthy Hollywood film producers would prefer to take their own Sphinx to Egypt, rather than use the old one! Day is made to look like night. In common film industry parlance, it is known as 'Day for Night'. The concept fascinated François Truffaut[4] so much that he made a film titled *Day for Night* (1973) as a tribute to the people who create films. Truffaut's film won the Academy award in 1973 for the Best Foreign Language Film.

More than half a century ago, the Western Ghats near Khandala doubled for the distant Kumaon hills recreating the sequence for *Madhumati*. That is not all; I learnt much later that almost 80 per cent of the film had to be re-shot in locations around Maharashtra. As a result, the production went over budget. It would have been a very serious financial situation for both *Madhumati* and Baba had it not been for a Good Samaritan who bailed them out. That incredible story deserves a chapter to itself.

THE MADHUMATI ENIGMA

Madhumati continues to raise awkward questions even after the passage of half a century. It is still a celluloid enigma. Wild speculations followed the release of the film on 19 September 1958. Why did a neo-realist film-maker of Bimal Roy's stature stoop to make a 'ghost' story, as many perceived *Madhumati*. The question remains unanswered to date.

The original synopsis of the film, used as publicity material in 1958, has been included in this book. But the dry literal prose fails to do justice to the complex structure of the film. We are thrown back to the question: Is *Madhumati* a romantic love story? Or is it a suspense thriller? It is important to bear in mind that over the years, the film has also earned a reputation of being the definitive tale of reincarnation. Some even go so far as to call it the mother of all reincarnation films. Without doubt it is all this but a great deal remains unexplained. So how does one begin to narrate the story of *Madhumati*? I shall make a sincere attempt to unravel some of these mysteries with the help of those who have studied the film. And in that process, I may even succeed in brushing aside some of the cobwebs around it.

True to the genre of a classic ghost story, *Madhumati* is a nocturnal tale. It begins on a dark night lashed by torrential rain and thunder. The opening shot of a desolate and spectral mansion, silhouetted against streaks of lightning brings to mind Kamal Amrohi's celebrated work, *Mahal* (1949). Inclement weather, rain, thunder, a dark lonely night, creates the ambience, the perfect mood for a ghost story narration. In the opening shot of *Mahal*, its protagonist (played by Ashok Kumar) is shown knocking the door of a deserted Gothic mansion. In *Madhumati* too, the protagonist knocks on a massive door to take shelter but the similarity between the two films ends after that.

After the Bimal Roy Production clock tower logo fades out and the film credits roll past, a large, black Dodge appears on the screen, flashing its blinding headlights. Exterior shots of the car are cut with close-ups of protagonist Dilip Kumar. The actor plays double role—as Devendra and Anand. With him in the car is a doctor friend. Suddenly their car is blocked by a landslide on that stormy night. Devendra and his friend are forced to take shelter in an abandoned mansion. They knock on its massive door but no one seems to respond. Looking around, Devendra finds a chord hanging by the door and tugs at it. A soft musical chime sounds and the door creaks open, revealing a gloomy, desolate interior. Devendra's friend asks him incredulously, 'How did you know there was a chord for the doorbell?'

Devendra answers absentmindedly: 'I somehow knew it was there.'

The two men step into the deserted mansion, led by a man as ancient as the mansion.

The interior of the mansion brings Devendra face to face with the fragments of an unfinished business. A dusty portrait of its erstwhile owner Ugranarayan forces Devendra to recognize his own brush strokes and he is thrown back to his past life. The narration begins to unfold in earnest as the lace curtain, gently swaying, opens up the flood gates of Devendra's recollections. He begins to recount his past life with these words: *'Mujhe yaad aa raha hai—saaf saaf yaad aa raha hai.'* (I am starting to remember…remember clearly).

And soft footfalls echo in his memory. As the film goes into flashback, weaving a fine tapestry of a past life narrative, it begins to dwell lovingly on the time when Devendra (Anand in his previous life), had come to these very hills as a manager for Ugranarayan's Shyamgarh Timber Estate. The entire narrative is in flashback, from Devendra's point of view. He narrates the story to a one-man audience, his doctor-friend. Within the flashback are structured other stories of love, betrayal, exploitation, land grabbing, crime and retribution.

THE ETERNAL LOVE STORY

If I simply surmise that in the Bimal Roy film repertory, *Madhumati* is the closest to a linear boy meets girl story, I would be ignoring its layered depth and larger concerns. It is true to an extent that the film explores the many splendoured stages of falling in love. Critic Maithili Rao believes it does:

'Though *Madhumati* has a complicated structure of reincarnation, look-alikes and mysterious apparitions, Roy lingers over the process of falling in love, the sweet nothings

of enchanted lovers, the trust and temptation that colour
their trysts. Even though a certain old fashioned decorum
reigns over these meetings, the exuberant folk song expresses
the ecstatic pleasure of love's sting.'

Falling in love, pleasing courtship, followed by wrenching
separation and the wheel turning a full circle before reinventing
itself with the story of reincarnation! All these constitute
Madhumati's layered journey.

The idea of time—both past and present—plays a crucial
part in the *Madhumati* narrative. These two entities fuse
seamlessly by the reincarnation-love story. The film's soundtrack
resonates with the sound of chiming clocks that mark the hour
8 pm repeatedly. In fact it is a dramatically important moment
in *Madhumati*. Devendra walks into the crumbling old mansion
at this hour; it was at 8 pm that *Madhumati* was lured into the
landlord's mansion in his previous life. Later in the narration, it
is at 8 pm once again when *Madhumati's* spirit returns to
encounter her tormentor, the powerful Ugranarayan. Time is
imperative in the film's narrative. And the notion of the two
merging, time past and time present remind me of T.S. Eliot's
memorable lines:

'Time present and time past
Are both perhaps present in time future,
And time future contained in time past.
If all time is eternally present
All time is unredeemable.
What might have been is an abstraction
Remaining a perpetual possibility
Only in a world of speculation.'

Burnt Norton—Four Quartets collection

In fact the very first line spoken in *Madhumati*, alludes to time.
'What time is it?' asks the anxious Devendra.

'Ten past eight.'

On hearing this, a visibly agitated Devendra, orders the driver: 'We have twenty miles to go! *Arrey jaldi chalao bhai, jaldi chalao.*' (Drive faster).

Reference to time is imaged innovatively, for example, the tribal woman Madhumati measures time by watching the length of the shadows on the ground or a rock without the help or knowledge of a watch or clock. The lengthening shadow of the pine tree on a boulder marks the time for the secret tryst with her Babuji, Anand. The repeated reference to time in *Madhumati* was conceived with a dramatic purpose in mind. It is a precursor to the film's fantastic climax when Madhumati's apparition makes a chilling entry just as the huge wall clock strikes eight. It is a cinematic moment conceived with tremendous originality and visual power and in the manner it is executed has made *Madhumati* earn an unique position amongst other films of the same genre.

On the aesthetic front, repeated references to time created sweet pastoral images on the silver screen. Cameraman K.K. Jaiswal, Dilip Gupta's former student, mentioned about this particular segment watching *Madhumati* for the fourteenth time in the course of a week in Pune in 1958: 'How does the shadow of the tree remain at the same place? I realized then that the scene had been shot indoors. But what perfection of lighting!'

A FINELY EXECUTED CLIMAX

I have serious doubts if the story-teller Bimal Roy was ever attracted to the conventional boy meets girl love story format or that he aspired to be the king of romance. Nonetheless a romantic at heart, love and romance feature significantly in all his films. In *Madhumati*, romance enhanced a cleverly crafted tale, invested with deep, understated humanism. But allow me to revert to the idea that its makers conceived *Madhumati* as a commercial, and not artistic enterprise. Maithili Rao[5] makes a pertinent case[6]:

'Arguably, *Madhumati* is Bimal Roy's most commercially designed production. Yet the film deconstructs many of the stereotyped images and notions of conventional, oft-repeated romantic tales between a village girl, the much hyped village belle of Hindi cinema, and a city babu/ gentleman. What Roy does in the process of reinventing is to discover new templates in that genre. *Madhumati's* magnificent and innovative finale, the subtle conflict of the real and fake, has been picked up by countless Bollywood films—most notably, *Om Shanti Om*. The seemingly implausible tale became convincing with Roy's restrained delicate narrative. To the oft-told tale of *pardesi-babu* and the village belle, Roy brings a sense of love's abiding wonder. He depicts the love between Anand and Madhu as an elemental force of nature, as delicate and inevitable as the unfurling of a wild mountain flower and as precipitous as a fall from a cliff and as enchanting as the song of a shy wood sprite waiting for her true love while she sings *Aaja re pardesi*…Madhu teases the viewer and Anand, allowing us a glimpse and then melting into the mist, like a lovely spirit from another world. Roy plays a variation of an old theme, of the hero's first sight of the beloved. It is both a beginning and the culmination of a quest.'

As the narrative progresses, Ugranarayan stumbles on a lovers' tryst in the forest glade. His black heart is captivated by the ravishing Madhumati being wooed by Anand, provoking resentment, envy and bitter class hatred. Dark thoughts spill over and drive him to pre-meditated crime. He makes a devious plan. Ordering Anand to leave town he gets his booze-loving servant, Charandas, stupidly drunk. The thorns thus removed, it is easy to trap the vulnerable, young Madhumati into the spider's web under the false pretext that the injured Anand is lying at his mansion. Hearing this news Madhumati naturally rushes into the well-planned trap and realizes her folly too late.

She puts up a brave front but is outwitted and in a futile attempt to escape, she falls to her death from the roof top. Like many unfortunate women in our culture, she has no choice but to embrace death in the face of dishonour. Anwesha Arya[7] reminds us:

> 'When Madhumati from the past flings herself, freeing herself, preserving her honour—the only way our unfortunate women are taught we can, by pelting down from the pinnacle of fear and plunging to her horrific end, it is that unpleasant silence after the relentless tinkling, jingle-jangle of those crazed bells on her running feet that the onlooker remembers. That final, deathly silence!'

That terrible moment of Madhumati's tragic death is one of the most poignantly imaged sequences of *Madhumati*. Her tragic death brings to close the love story chapter of the film. From that point the film is dominated by a sense of gloomy tragedy. Overwhelmed by grief, Anand quits Ugranarayan's job, but hangs around, waiting for an opportunity to collect enough evidence to convict the killer. And his opportunity comes in an unexpected twist in the story. Roaming with his sketch pad in the forest glades, Anand accidentally comes across a woman who has an uncanny resemblance to Madhumati. Startled by Madhavi's splitting image of Madhumati and her physical resemblance to his beloved, Anand goes to the extent of accusing the poor Madhavi of playing games with him!

Introducing the look-alike was a clever cinematic ploy. It paved the way to construct the master stroke for the film's climax when Madhavi impersonates Madhumati in an attempt to unmask Ugranarayan and force a confession. Anand is confident that Ugranarayan would blurt out his guilty secret on seeing his dead victim. And thus, a fantastic plan is hatched—Madhavi dressed as Madhu appears at the appointed hour at

Ugranarayan's mansion. What happens next is beyond anyone's wildest expectations. The viewer is gently led up the garden path to a grand finale intended to leave everyone gasping for breath.

On the appointed night, Madhavi's team is delayed by a fierce storm. Inside the mansion, Anand pretends to paint Ugranarayan's portrait. As the clock strikes eight, the vast mansion is plunged in darkness. In the dark gloom, punctuated by streaks of lightning, the figure of Madhumati emerges, her eyes glazed, her face stripped of emotion. She approaches her killer and reminds him of his heinous crime. Anand believes their plan to be moving as intended. All of a sudden the fake Madhu, or Madhavi, arrives in a police platoon. On screen the twin images of Madhumati appear like a double vision. Only then does Anand realize that the spirit of the dead Madhu had stepped in to give evidence of the grisly crime. Caught between the real and unreal, the spirit and the flesh, Anand follows Madhu's spirit up the stairs and falls to his death from the roof top, in the manner of his beloved. The lovers are reunited, life after life. Cinematographer Dilip Gupta has left a factual account of how they achieved this effect on screen:

> 'There is a scene where Madhumati and the look-alike come together and one of them fades out. This was done by masking. It was not a special effect done optically. It was done by using a mask at the matte box. I did it myself. The timing of the artiste's movement had to be perfect. The very first take was OK!'

It is in its cleverly written climax that *Madhumati* excels in ingenuity and plausibility rather than in sensation and morbid horror. A marvellous triumph of technology, achieved without special effects or cinematic gimmicks! Sound and light effects build up the spooky ambience. Dilip Kumar's suggestion to include the meowing of a cat (that I had overheard as a girl), may not have been added, but there is a quick cut of the black canine whining, portending sinister omens. The image and sound builds up the supernatural effect of the situation. I was not surprised to hear Clare Wilkinson-Weber[8] commenting that she finds the idea of Madhumati's spirit stalking Ugranarayan a chilling film experience:

> 'I have always found it quite chilling the moment one realizes that the woman stalking Ugranarayan is not the woman hired to play the part but instead Madhumati herself. I think that being in black and white adds greatly to the disturbing final scenes, which I think is an artifact of viewing it today in a world where we've become so accustomed to colour films. It's rather like discovering an old film or faded photograph that contains a long buried secret (just as of course the drawings at the beginning of the film are the beginning of the revelation of the secret of Madhumati's murder). Bimal Roy couldn't have anticipated the aesthetic effects of black and white on a 2012 viewer—however, the complex time shifts in the film are, I feel, very purposeful, and add a great deal of atmosphere to the film. The nesting of the stories within each other gives a rather ethereal feel to the entire film, another factor that contributes to the "frisson" of the scene in which Madhumati gets her revenge.'

OTHER CONCERNS

Devendra lapses into silence as the flashback concludes. The story limps back to time present. In his present life Anand has been reborn as Devendra; his wife Radha is Madhumati reborn. That takes care of the reincarnation angle of the story. Sonja Majumder in her essay, 'Revisiting Madhumati'[9] draws attention to some of the lesser known features of the film by the following observations:

'Roy's genuine concerns for the marginalized sections of society, their vulnerability and his damnation of social injustice are reflected vividly in *Madhumati*. A rigid social hierarchy is shown to flourish with its ugly excesses. Ugranarayan's timber estate runs on feudal principles. Subordinates have no rights. They are at the mercy of superiors who treat them with contempt. People with superior social standing abuse their powers, worse still, the one at the top of this hierarchy, Ugranarayan, deems himself above the law. The question of exploitation is not restricted to class alone, but it exists in regard to the relationship between representing the so-called mainstream society, and the tribal community to which Madhumati belongs.'

I agree with Sonja's interpretation about my father's larger social concerns manifesting themselves even in a film declared his most commercial work. In *Madhumati*, he did not lose sight of the ground reality and inequitable social patterns. My visit to the Ranikhet region was an eye opener. I was shocked to realize the extent of the forest mafia's successful invasion into this beautiful region who had burnt and looted vast tracts of forest land, ravaged villages, leaving tell-tale signs, and no doubt abused the women of the area. In *Madhumati*, Baba's concern for the marginalized sections, particularly those dependent on the forest resources for a livelihood is narrated through nuanced subplots. Ugranarayan's character points clearly to a land grabber, present-day builders, and the timber mafia wreaking havoc in the hills. The abuse of vulnerable sections including women is part of that scheme. All these aspects are hinted at in *Madhumati*.

The scene depicting confrontation between Madhu's father, Paan Raja, and Anand is noteworthy in this regard. Paan Raja perceives Anand as the outsider—the exploiter class. He accuses Anand of complicity and falsehood. Fortunately for him, and for us, none of Bimal Roy's heroes fit the part of an exploitative male. And Anand is no exception. The innocent Madhu is not duped or deserted by the *pardesi-babu*, her city lover which is the run of the mill staple in Hindi cinema. Anand would have honourably married Madhu. It is, in fact, the gutsy Madhu who takes the initiative of carrying her love into several lives. The other important part is Madhu's character. She is not portrayed as a helpless, coy, pallu-chewing village belle typified in mainstream liaisons of cross-cultural romance. Madhu is fearless and intelligent, with deer-like instincts—quite the opposite of village belles of conventional Hindi cinema.

A STORY TO END ALL STORIES

Writer Ritwick Kumar Ghatak's *Madhumati* is a fantastic tale of the unexpected—a melodramatic saga intended to click at the box-office. It was a sharp departure from the stark social realism for which both the writer and director Bimal Roy were celebrated, prompting curious reactions from many including Meghnad Desai who asked: 'Tell me; was *Madhumati* perhaps inspired by Tagore's *Hungry Stones* (*Ksudito Pashan*) or Kamal Amrohi's *Mahal*? It is a transitional film for your father—unlike any other Bimal Roy work. The story too is so untypical of writer Ghatak.'

Director Tigmanshu Dhulia quizzed me: 'Is it true that Ghatak wrote *Madhumati* on a small chit of paper?'

Unable to contain my own curiosity, I called Surama, Ghatak's widow, in August 2010, wondering if she could shed any light on what could have prompted her renowned husband to write a spooky tale, leaving behind an unsolved riddle. Surama Ghatak did not remember much, though she did recall that originally, the opening scene was conceived quite differently:

'Ritwick did not want to expose the faces of the two protagonists at the beginning of the story. The idea was not to reveal their identity. It was to be disclosed at the end of the past-life flashback. They start narrating their past life story, faces in silhouette. At the end of the flashback, two blossoms float from either side to meet mid-stream to convey eternal, deathless love. At the end of the story, the speakers' faces are visible…and the spectators realize that the narrators and the protagonists are one. The reunion at the train station was not in the original version written by Ghatak.'

The final words in this chapter on the curious story of *Madhumati*, belong to the maverick writer Ritwick Kumar Ghatak. The day his story was confirmed by director Bimal Roy for the princely sum of three hundred rupees, he squatted as usual under the nameless tree of Mohan Studios where BRP unit members played their inveterate carrom games. Inhaling a beedi deeply, Ghatak paused to brag to all within earshot: 'I have written such a f***ing ghost story for that b…dy capitalist named Bimal Roy, it will demolish him for good!'

Ritwick Kumar Ghatak has left us a mystery yet unsolved, though his tale has certainly been worth telling.

Madhumati remains the biggest grosser of all Baba's works. It continues to enthrall audiences the world over. Offers to colourize the film or have it staged on London's West End continue to overwhelm and thrill us.

However, it is not the end of the story!

The film ran for twenty-four weeks in Bombay's Roxy cinema, beginning 19 September 1958, and just a week short of its silver jubilee it was taken off. According to the film's editors Das and Sakharam, it was withdrawn for a strange reason. Yet another story waiting to be written; meanwhile the journey into the hills beckons us…

As I conclude, Aditi Sen's response to the film draws my attention. Her thoughts still hold true for many: 'When it is pouring outside, I want to rewind to...*Madhumati* where the climax is undoubtedly disturbing and powerful but to me [sic] the appeal of *Madhumati* is very different. No matter how often I watch it the goose-bumps return...'

NOTES

[1]Deep Bhatt was born in 1963 in the Himalayan region. His magnificent obsession for cinema has made him a film journalist. This is both a hobby as well as a livelihood. Currently, he is writing a book on cinema in society and a second one on actor Dev Anand. Deep believes Bimal Roy helped him understand cinema and society. He is a senior journalist at *Hindustan Times* (Hindi edition) from Haldwani and also contributes to the *Hindustan Times* Magazine *Kadambini* and the magazine *Samkaleen Teesri Duniya*.

[2]The quotes from Dilip Gupta and K.K. Jaiswal have been included with the kind permission of Champa Roy from her book *The Portrait of Dilip Gupta: The Artist Who Painted with Light and Shade*. (Published by Champa Roy, 2010)

[3]George Mikes (15 February 1912–30 August 1987) was a Hungarian-born British author, best known for his humorous commentaries on various countries. He authored the famous books *How to be an Alien, Land of the Rising Yen* and *How to Scrape Skies*, among other delightful titles.

[4]François Truffaut (6 February 1932–21 October 1984) was an influential film-maker and film critic—one of the founders of the French New Wave Cinema. In a film career lasting over a quarter of a century, he remains an icon of the French film industry. He was also a screenwriter, producer and actor, working on over twenty-five films.

[5]See list of contributors.

[6]For further reading: Maithili Rao's essay 'Idealized Women and a Realist's Eye' from *The Man Who Spoke in Pictures*, edited by Rinki Roy Bhattacharya (Penguin Books, 2009).

[7]See list of contributors.

[8]See list of contributors.

[9]For further reading: Sonja Majumder's essay 'Revisiting *Madhumati*' from *The Man Who Spoke in Pictures* edited by Rinki Bhattacharya (Penguin Books, 2009).

3

Recasting

Pre-imagining is the imagining of things which are to be...
—Leonardo Da Vinci,
Fogli B.2v.

It was 25 June and we would finally be on our much awaited trip to Ranikhet that afternoon. Maithili and I checked into the Indigo flight to Delhi. The next phase was to board the Kathgodam Express that night from Old Delhi Railway Station—an experience that could be 'overwhelming' warned my friend Mala. As we checked in, my thoughts dwelt on what an incredible adventure it must have been for a film crew fifty-four years ago. A three-phase journey—first from Bombay to Lucknow (Delhi, in our case); then to Kathgodam and finally up the hills. It must have been adventurous as well as arduous for an entire film unit, loaded with heavy equipment, the cast and technicians in tow. I could not figure out why Baba had selected a location so far away from civilization when he had other choices! But there was no one to answer me. I must have given up at some point, the gentle movement of the plane rocking me into slumber. In that half-awake state, I ruminated on the birth of the *Madhumati* book.

The whole thing started with the uneasy sensation that I experienced visiting the ageing actor Pran in April 2008. The book was then nowhere on the agenda. It was only much later that I understood why Pran's helpless appearance had haunted me for days. It was a sensation of loss and foreboding that inspired me to write the book. Taking full advantage of being Bimal Roy's eldest daughter, I had scribbled small notes to the three leading *Madhumati* stars with a single request worded in the manner of an SOS: 'Talk to me, tell me how this film was made, tell me all that you remember.' I was tempted to write the desperate words, 'Before it is too late,' but resisted.

I had easy access to all the three thespians as well as others who worked with Baba. Living in the vicinity of Pali Hill was another advantage. I am separated from Dilip Kumar and Pran-Sahab by a few furlongs. Notes followed calls, and visits followed other notes. The first response came surprisingly from Chennai. The film's heroine, Vyjayanthimala's charming reply thrilled me: 'It is many decades since *Madhumati* was made, Rinki. Of course I was a part of that great film and worked with your illustrious father. I can answer only some of your questions as best as I remember…'

Elated by her assurance, I considered writing an entire chapter on how Baba chose his actors; recast them, reinventing their screen images with his eye for detail. Evidently, he had a fairly accurate idea of how his films should appear. He had a flair, a distinct clarity of vision to intuitively pick actors who would live their part rather than merely play it. Regardless of whether the actors were renowned or new comers, he knew the importance of imaging a character and understood that it was critical to create a world that exists nowhere except in the mind of the maker before finding itself on the silver screen. Robert Bresson, the New Wave French director, had put it bluntly: 'My movie is born first in my head and dies on paper.'

Films can die on paper unless the myth, the make-belief world its director aspires to capture, is rendered credible. This was especially true of *Madhumati* where reality, as we understand, takes a back seat and pure fantasy is at the forefront. The entire onus of taking the narration forward after all, rests as much on the director and his technical crew, as on the actors. The selection of actors can make or mar a film!

An incident relating to the casting of Baba's debut film, *Udayer Pathe* comes to mind. For a long time, no suitable heroine was found to play the female lead, Gopa. Noted stars and new comers were shortlisted but rejected. One morning, a skinny, nondescript young woman walked into the New Theatres Studio, ostensibly to audition for playback singing. Her flute-like voice impressed the studio bosses, including my father, who happened to be on the selection panel. The very next morning baba announced that his search for the *Udayer Pathe* heroine had ended; he had discovered Gopa in the skinny singer, Binata Bose.

His extraordinary decision provoked a huge amount of skepticism; many considered it foolhardy, but he stood firm. And the unknown woman in the pivotal female lead soon proved critics wrong with her peerless rendition of Gopa. Baba also flouted the prevailing norms by casting the one-film old Radhamohan Bhattacharya who had played a villain earlier, as the romantic hero. His debut film *Udayer Pathe* had a record run for a full year at Kolkata's Chitra cinema. Equally well-known is the fact that it went on to become a cult film, revolutionizing the profile of Indian cinema. The film set a new cinematic template that inspired a host of young Bengalis to make films. Notable among them were Satyajit Ray, working as a commercial artist with Signet Press, Mrinal Sen, Ritwick Ghatak, Tapan Sinha and others.

A similar situation recurred in 1953 when Ashok Kumar

was planning *Parineeta*. The Ashok Kumar–Nalini Jaywant pair
was considered big box-office bait of the period. I remember
hearing that producer Ashok Kumar, also the hero, was keen
that Baba consider Nalini Jaywant in the role of Lalita.
Meanwhile, a dainty newcomer called Meena Kumari had come
for an audition to Bombay Talkies and Baba happened to see
her. He had found the perfect Lalita in Meena Kumari. *Parineeta*
rates high amongst Meena Kumari's flawless works. The film
firmly established the Ashok Kumar–Meena Kumari romantic
lead who starred in several films after the phenomenal success of
Parineeta.

Another interesting casting story is about Bollywood's original
muscle man, Dharmendra. This story is of a more recent origin.
The Adonis like Dharmendra had turned up to find work at the
BRP office, like many aspiring hopefuls of the time. But
Dharmendra was more fortunate. He received one hundred
rupees as a signing amount and put on hold for a future Bimal
Roy film. That film, to Dharmendra's good fortune, turned out
to be the memorable *Bandini*. With that film, a star was born.
The self-effacing and unobtrusive, Bimal Roy was a phenomenal
casting guru!

IMAGING THROUGH THE REALIST'S EYE

With an enviable track record for impeccable casting and his
eye for detail, Baba accomplished astonishing results—his casting
of Nutan for *Sujata* (1959) and *Bandini*, for example was
outstanding. The incomparable Nutan has always appeared
divine, confessed the thespian Naseeruddin Shah. Shah drew
attention to Sunil Dutt's brilliant performance as Adhir, the
idealist romantic who falls in love with a dalit woman in *Sujata*.
'It was the most understated role in Sunil Dutt's entire acting
career,' observed Shah.

Personally, I rate Baba's casting of Motilal as Devdas's mentor Chunilal, a coup par excellence. I doubt if any one can dispute this claim or improve upon Motilal's extraordinary performance.

The story-teller in Baba could intuitively sense an actor's potential ability to sculpt characters. Jonathan Demme, director of the brilliant film *Philadelphia* (1993) is reported to have said: 'All the great actors are great story tellers. They have to be.'

He elaborates further in *The New York Times*[1] with reference to actor Denzel Washington: 'We prepare the production and set up the shots, but then the camera is rolling and it is the actors who are telling the story of the movie.'

Many of Baba's stars give him credit for extracting flawless performances. They felt secure in the belief he could make them blossom on the screen. Indeed baba got the best out of his actors. But it was always a two-way street. His actors were inspired to maximize their ability 'to tell the story' as Demme believed. There can be no doubt that films like *Sujata* and *Bandini* were impossible without Nutan. For that matter, *Do Bigha Zamin* would have been downright ordinary without actor Balraj Sahni as the peasant protagonist Shambhu Mahato. Interestingly, off-screen, Balraj Sahni was always a picture of suaveness, dressed impeccably in western-style clothes.

In the days of Guru Dutt, Mehboob Khan and Bimal Roy, casting directors were unknown. Like many of his contemporaries, decisions about the film's star cast or composers rested with my father. *Devdas* (1955) was yet another casting coup. Until Bengal's leading female star, the divine Suchitra Sen was signed as Parvati, Bengali female stars were rarely seen on the Hindi cinema screen. Though there were at least half a dozen Bengali heroes commanding top billing in Bombay since the mid-1930s. Notable amongst them were Ashok Kumar Ganguly and his gifted younger brother Kishore Kumar besides Pradeep Kumar. Other cameo actors from Bengal like Keshto Mukherjee, Asit Sen and Utpal Dutt deserve mention.

And until *Devdas*, the Dilip Kumar–Vyjayanthimala combination had never been paired and their magnificent screen chemistry in this film prompted no less than six films together[2] including *Madhumati*. Curious to discover the reason for Baba repeating the Devdas pair, I asked Baba's assistant Debu Sen who confirmed that the original casting for *Madhumati* included Dilip Kumar and Vyjayanthimala. An interview with Dilip Kumar confirmed this further:

> 'Bimalda had already formed a silhouette of *Madhumati* in his mind and briefly touched upon it as we concluded work on *Devdas*. And later, when he gave me his first narration in the company of writer Ritwik Ghatak, I could sense his confidence in the subject, even though several people had expressed misgivings about its metaphysical layers, not easy for the average viewer to absorb. Though the concept of reincarnation and the audience's inability to identify with it was a latent fear, we worked with the common objective of taking the film to box office success.'

From the start, it appears Baba had formatted a populist formula adopted by mainstream practitioners of that era to structure *Madhumati*. It consisted of a single romantic pair (much before multiple pairs became the trend), a teeth-gnashing villain, the hero's comic sidekick, and of course, the ubiquitous and stern father of the heroine. Baba conformed to this populist pattern, casting Vyjayanthimala, Dilip Kumar, Pran and Johnny Walker in the pivotal roles—and yet this improbable tale of rebirth bore the stamp of the stylist renowned for his restraint, his realism.

Dilip Kumar, the undisputed king of women's hearts, was tailor made to play the nuanced, romantic screen-lover Anand. But before he essayed the easy-going Anand, the actor had to systematically erase his long standing image as Bollywood's tragedy king. Female fans had long been slaves to Dilip Kumar's screen persona of an intense, darkly brooding man. Razia Husain relates the excitement in her teenaged heart when she met the man of her dreams shooting for *Madhumati* in Ghorakhal:

> 'After completing the shot they (Bimalda and Dilip Kumar) came over and we were introduced to them. I remember my face turning red and a feeling of awkwardness on seeing him in person. In those days actors were invisible. One could only worship them from afar on cinema posters and magazines and of course in the movie halls. Never in human form. And so my heart was going boom-boodi-boom. Remember, I was only a shy teenager with a huge crush on Dilip Sahab. He was the first love of my entire life of fourteen years!'

If we rewind to some of his celebrated titles from the 1950s, Dilip Kumar had repeatedly played the tragic lover film after film. Mehboob Khan's *Andaaz* (1949), Kidar Sharma's *Jogan* (1950), Nitin Bose's *Deedar* (1951) and Amiya Chakravarty's *Daag* (1952), are all cases in point where he essays a man destined to suffer great personal tragedy.

The buoyant, carefree Anand, treading lightly through an ethereal landscape with a song in his heart, presented just the opposite image. It was an unusually relaxed Dilip Kumar in *Madhumati*. Lip-syncing Mukesh's evergreen rendition *Suhana safar aur yeh mausam haseen*, Anand's introduction etches an iconic screen moment. With effortless ease, Dilip Kumar breezes in translating the blithe spirit of poet Shailendra's lyrical words, paying homage to the beauty of a charmed journey in a perfect season.

Towards the end of *Madhumati*, Anand's character undergoes a dramatic change. His beloved Madhu's tragic death is a shattering blow. It sends the quintessential romantic hero into a decline and the easy-going Anand turns into an obsessive, melancholic man. In the latter part of the film Anand, in the manner of *Devdas*, cannot reconcile to his beloved's loss. Though he does not take to the bottle as companion, he descends speedily into loneliness and grim self-reproach; no other actor could portray the pain of a traumatized lover, a screen persona Dilip Kumar had perfected long before *Madhumati*. The portrait of the carefree Anand was a new avatar of Dilip Kumar, and being the seasoned actor that he was, he played the two sides of Anand's personality with equal aplomb.

A tad tentatively, I asked the star, 'What prompted you to accept *Madhumati*?'

His reply was spontaneous:

'My eagerness to work again with Bimal Roy after the rich experience we shared during the making of *Devdas*. Bimalda and I shared a bond of mutual respect and affection. It began long before we came together for *Devdas*. While every role I played had its distinct merits and provocations, *Madhumati* had the added incentive of the construction of the narrative and the layers of unpredictability in it.'

THAT FIRST GLIMPSE

Maithili Rao confirms the astute story-teller in my father: 'As a good story-teller, in Roy's films, our first sight of the protagonist is a dramatic event.'

Madhumati is replete with dramatic, bewitching and at times, comic moments when the story's characters are introduced. One scene that tugs at my visual memory is the droll entry of Anand's man servant, Charandas. Instructed to receive his new master (Anand) at the railway station, the booze-loving Charan gets hopelessly drunk and forgets where he was supposed to go. Anand reaches a crossroad and perplexed, decides to toss a coin to decide which way to follow. But the tossed coin does not find its way to the ground. Amazed, he looks up to find a man hanging upside down bat-like from a tree. This strange character has the gall to accost his boss with these comical lines punning on the word *'anand'*: *'Aap neeche anand toh main upper anand!'* (If you are happy down there, I am happy up here).

Charan's comic introduction never fails to raise delightful chuckles. The actor with the rather odd on-screen name Johnny Walker (named after the popular Scotch whiskey brand) specialized in playing the inebriated underdog, the typical comic-relief in film after film. And yet Badruddin Qazi[3] (his actual name) never drank a drop in his life. Putting a jigsaw puzzle in place has never been my forte but some pieces did click into position when R.S. Pant said that the village fair in the film and the scene in which Johnny Walker hangs upside down from a tree were shot in the vicinity of the cross roads approaching the now famous Ghorakhal Sainik School.

As unforgettable is the moment when *Madhumati* bewitchingly glides onto the screen, a vision of radiant pastoral beauty, framed against silver streaks of a cascading waterfall, her image is revealed to viewer's from Anand's point of view. The viewer is allowed just a glimpse of the as yet un-named, mysterious and sensuous creature. Intriguingly visible one moment, she vanishes from sight in the very next frame and in an endless series of tantalizing catch-me-if-you-can shots, the film eloquently establishes the romantic pair. The song sequence when the viewer first sights this ravishing hill beauty is the precise moment when the film's theme itself is revealed hauntingly in the wistful song *Aaja re, main toh kabse khari is paar*. The tender, erotic words speak of an ancient, endless wait of the weary and parched beloved longing for her *pardesi* (stranger) lover—poised across the chasm of timeless separation. The song teases the viewer and Anand alike with its mysterious yet eloquent words.

Living up to her director's high expectations, Vyjayanthimala was sensational as the radiant Madhumati. If she had felt justly rewarded playing the mature Chandramukhi, the actress felt abundantly fulfilled playing the bubbly, innocent Madhumati. For Vyjayanthimala, it was an incredible high when director Bimal Roy signed her as Chandramukhi in *Devdas*:

> 'The news was like manna from heaven! Not in my wildest dreams had I imagined that a great, serious film-maker like Bimal Roy would think of casting me for the role of Chandramukhi in his *Devdas*. People from the film industry and outside it acclaimed my work. Initially I was very much in awe of Bimalda and spared no effort to satisfy my director by playing Chandramukhi. The character demanded histrionics and the film became a turning point in my career. It was the first time that I played a serious role, different from any of my other films where dance always overshadowed the actress. Playing Chandramukhi under Bimalda's direction gave me the scope to display my dramatic talent as a serious actress. *Devdas* was a unique experience for me.'

Another thrillingly scripted, powerfully imaged first sight of a character in *Madhumati* was the confrontational scene when Ugranarayan makes his tumultuous entry on horseback. Dr Razia Husain vividly remembers the shooting of this dramatic sequence:

> 'An entire hillside was set up with jhoolas and little shops. The crowd was local, agog with curiosity to see the shooting. There was an air of festivity and excitement. People came from all over. The long shots of the mela were canned. A "double" on horseback came charging down the hillside simulating Pran, the villain of the film. The crowd ran about and dispersed spontaneously, so the shot did not require a retake.'

Ugranarayan storms into the frame raising dust and chaos through the milling crowds in a narrow village alley. On his unstoppable track, a little boy was almost trampled under his horse. Outraged by the man's ruthless behaviour, Anand confronts the powerful landlord and at once hailed a local hero. After this, Madhumati does not shy away from the stranger but begins to view him with sympathy.

Ugranarayan's inauspicious entry presages evil into the narrative. Portrayed as a suave, urbane man, the tyrannical landlord dominates his serene sylvan estate, treating it as his personal fiefdom. Observing the manner in which director Bimal Roy paints his villains, noted actor Naseeruddin Shah observes:

> 'Roy's choice of stories illustrates his deep compassion for and understanding of the plight of the less privileged, and the antagonists in his films are not the teeth-gnashing villainous ogres of yore but the genteel landed aristocracy turned into champion hypocrites by the positions of power they occupy.'[4]

Naseeruddin Shah himself had essayed the genteel, aristocratic villain, the character of the soft-spoken poet Gulfam Hassan whose public persona is an elegant front for gun-running in the John Matthew Matthan film, *Sarfarosh* (1999)[5]. Yet another remarkable portrayal of the gentleman-villain in more recent times is of the wily landlord, Ramadhin Singh in *Gangs of Wasseypur* (2012), played by the gifted film-maker, Tigmanshu Dhulia[6] with nerve-chilling composure. Alternative cinema has made honest attempts in the works of Satyajit Ray, Shyam Benegal and Anurag Kashyap, to image the duality of men and women posing as sensitive individuals with dubious social aspirations. The Ramadhirs and the Gulfams are examples of what Shah scathingly refers to as villains from the 'mileau of genteel landed aristocracy'. These images are not the archetypal Bollywood manufactured teeth-gnashing baddies. They are real, and therefore more menacing. The point is, *Madhumati,* recognized as Bimal Roy's most commercial film, was structured with a realist's eye. His characters emerge from the realm of reality; his vision and his deep compassion, his concern about India's social reality was never compromised at the altar of mainstream cinema.

Another important example of Bimal Roy's eye for realistic rendering was the manner in which he imaged *Madhumati*'s ghost. He scrupulously avoided the stereotype and chose to make her appear perfectly human. Clare's[7] observation emphasizes this aspect:

> '...(a)s I recall, the camera in the *Madhumati* ghost scene puts the door through which Madhumati emerges in the background to the left, and she sort of glides through it towards her victim. When the fake Madhumati rushes in late, she comes in the same door, in the same shot. I'm no expert on stagecraft but I sense that doing that in close up would not have worked. Having Madhumati emerge like that is a coup. But I might not be remembering it correctly...
> I was reminded also that it was clever that your Dad didn't film her as a stereotypical ghost, but as an ordinary woman, so that we'd have no idea that she was a ghost.'

TRIBUTE FROM HIS STARS

The many compliments showered on my father by his gifted galaxy of artists deserve mention. It is fitting to include them in this concluding part to a chapter highlighting the three *Madhumati* icons.

The Pran-Bimal Roy association went back to the early 1950s when both were at the peak of their professional life. They created memorable celluloid moments with *Biraj Bahu* (1954), *Devdas* and *Madhumati*.

A handsome man, many believe that Pran had the screen

image suited to play the romantic hero. He came to the forefront of Hindi cinema as a cheek-chewing villainous presence in modest Punjabi productions. His discovery one night at Lahore's infamous Heera Mandi neighbourhood—the city's red-light quarter, by writer Walli Mohammed Walli resulted in his being cast in a negative role in the 1940 Punjabi film *Yamla Jat*. The decision proved irreversible. A feeble attempt was made later to resurrect his image with a romantic role opposite the sensational singing icon, Noor Jehan. But Pran had been permanently marked as Indian cinema's original villain. Mothers, it is believed, refused to name their sons Pran.

The following anecdote is reconstructed from the titbits gleaned from the actor as he reminisced about a long gone sepia-stained era of Indian cinema: 'After the release of *Madhumati*, I was in Madras for the shooting of a new film. On the first day, I was introduced to the heroine from the south; the lady turned around and exclaimed "Oh! I know him very well; I have seen *Madhumati* thirty times!"'

Needless to say the actress may have been terrified—and Pran too, needless to say, must have worked his well-known charm to undo the damage his excellent portrayal of the terrifyingly primeval villain Ugranarayan may have created. He goes on to recount his experience of working with Bimal Roy, and the respect with which all actors were treated, whether they were celebrated stars or lowly extras. In particular he mentions the manner in which the director took trouble to fine tune his expectation from those he was working with to recreate and tell a story meaningfully:

'There is no other word for Bimalda but to say he was an utterly brilliant director. Bimalda was a soft spoken man, a gentleman; one of the finest directors with whom I have worked. On the sets, he would quietly tell the artistes what he wanted from them. He got the best out of us. *Madhumati*

is one of my favourite films. On the release of my biography
And Pran, I was gifted a portrait by Anjana Kuthiala. It
thrilled me that the artist had been inspired by my role in
Madhumati.'

Vyjayanthimala confirms *Madhumati*'s perennial charm as a
black and white classic and its iconic stature in her career. She
seems particularly averse to the idea of the film being colourized—
as is the current craze, to transform iconic black and white
celluloid classics into garish colourized versions for re-runs. The
most noteworthy example is the colourized version of K. Asif's
Mughal-e-Azam (1960).

> 'The success and impact of *Madhumati* was so great that to
> this day the film is evergreen. I think the film should never
> be coloured. *Madhumati* is beautiful, eerie and dramatic as
> it is. The deep impact it created in black and white sans
> gloss and glam. This will be lost in color. *Devdas* and
> *Madhumati* have been two of my most special films.'

Dilip Kumar has fond memories of being part of the *Madhumati*
team. He felt it had a clever and ingenious script even though he
had concerns about its commercial viability. And yet he lent his
support generously. He reflects on Baba, his director Bimalda,
with sincere admiration:

> 'Bimalda's direction gave me the pleasure of knowing a
> man who believed in perfection and hard work as much as
> I did. He appreciated my style of working, the pains I took
> to invest life into my characters. He helped his artistes
> understand his visualization of a scene or moment. In the
> very first draft of *Madhumati*, I could sense the script's
> possibilities. It appeared rather tricky for me to be the
> pivot of a suspenseful narrative that alternated between the
> past and present and constantly threw up gripping
> situations. None of my previous film-characters were

required to be connected to a life in a previous birth. That was tricky for me. More so, as my character was the pivot of the film's evolution and dramatic appeal. In my career of working in the Indian film industry, I would say without hesitation that *Devdas* and *Madhumati* took me to great heights as far as name, fame and acting was concerned.'

Dilip Kumar, one of Baba's favourite actors had a student-teacher bonding with his director. His unconditional respect for my father made him rally round the producer-director during a particularly bleak period after the completion of *Madhumati*. This episode is documented in the book's Afterword. The screen thespian pays him a heartfelt homage with these words: 'We did not have acting schools those days. But we had a director like Bimal Roy who gently took us under the skin of the character. In my formative years it was an education to work with him. I put Bimal Roy head and shoulders above his contemporaries. I miss him.'

Madhumati belongs to the Indian *Belle Époque*. In Bimal Roy's formidable repertory it remains his most watched and best loved work. The film is great fun to watch even after fifty-six years since it was first released. In this film Baba touched a new button, created an original template that tempted many other film-makers into imitating the supernatural genre. It is redundant to mention the several rebirth stories that have been made since. Considered the voice of social change for his generation, Baba briefly broke away from the serious tradition of humanism and social concerns he espoused in order to explore another genre of story-telling. And I think the entire crew and cast—including the very serious Bimal Roy—had a blast making *Madhumati*!

The Kathgodam Express slowly drew into the overcrowded Old Delhi Station. The coolie dumped our bags unceremoniously on the platform and vanished into the growing crowd. Unused to train travel, we surveyed our baggage, wondering whether we would manage to haul it up the unsteady steps of the bogie. We actually put up a creditable performance and after some confusion about our seat numbers, settled into narrow benches. What a strange, unfamiliar experience it was to spend the night in a Non-AC 3 Tier sleeper. I remember calling my daughter Anwesha in UK and laughing, 'Look what a spot Dadu's *Madhumati* has put me in! I am trying to fit myself on a berth that is too short for my long legs while the filthy toilets have not a drop of water.'

I hardly slept on the train as I kept wondering why Baba selected that long distance location…a journey across three states of India, taking over twenty-four hours. I could reach London faster… As we approached our destination, I received a text message from Deep Bhatt: 'Didi, please get down at Kathgodam and wait. We are coming. Regards.'

NOTES

[1] *The New York Times* International Weekly article published in *The Asian Age* on 29 September 2012, Page 7, titled: 'How the accidental actor does it' by Denzil Washington.

[2] B.R. Chopra's *Naya Daur* (1957), *Leader* (1964), *Paigham* (1959), Dilip Kumar's home production, *Gunga Jumna* (1961) and H.S. Rawail's *Sunghursh* (1968).

[3] Badruddin Qazi was given the screen name of Johnny Walker by his mentor Guru Dutt. The well-known comic actor impressed the latter by enacting a set piece, playing a drunk.

[4] Naseeruddin Shah is an actor and theatre director. He writes occasionally. Excerpt is taken from his article 'Actors in Bimal Roy's films'. In the book *Bimal Roy: The Man Who Spoke in Pictures*, ed. Rinki Roy Bhattacharya.

[5] *Sarfarosh* (1999), directed by John Matthew Matthan, starring Aamir Khan, Naseeruddin Shah, Sonali Bendre.

[6]Tigmanshu Dhulia, the gifted director of *Haasil* (2003), *Paan Singh Tomar* (2010) and other noteworthy films essays. Ramadhir Singh, the villain in the Anurag Kashyap film *Gangs of Wasseypur* (2012).

[7]See list of contributors.

4

Backstage Workers

Those of us who worked in cinema were deeply involved in our work. Directors, art directors, music directors, actors, all of us had a great sense of togetherness. I had a great pleasure in working with directors like Bimal Roy, P.C. Barua and Nitin Bose.

—Dilip Gupta

AT THE LOCATION

Deep Bhatt, his wife Hansi and their neighbour Mr Joshi had come by road from Haldwani to receive us at the Kathgodam Station. Our train reached before time, unusual for the Indian Railways! During the final phase of the train journey, Deep's text popped up every few minutes. I had not met Deep Bhatt, nor knew what he looked like. Both of us relied on our respective cell phones to aid us. After what seemed like an eternity in that dingy neon lit Kathgodam waiting room, his last text popped up: 'Didi, we are waiting outside the station, regards. Deep'.

As we stepped out of the cluttered station, right across the street I saw a youngish man in a Blue T-shirt looking at us intently. Had to be Deep Bhatt, I thought and I was right. We exchanged pleasantries on the street. When I saw the stationary car intended to drive us uphill 40 kilometres to Bhowali, my heart sank. None of us were slim, quite the contrary. And it is against my principle to travel light. Maithili and I had large bags with hand luggage to match. I began to worry how the three plump women would fit into the back seat. Somehow, all three, along with the hand luggage, managed to squeeze tightly into the back seat of the car. We rolled about like passengers on a ship in choppy waters as the car began to heave uphill. It was too early for tea shops to open but all of us ached for the first cup of chai.

Out of the blue, a tea stall beckoned us. Salvi, an en route place seemed like a popular stop. From the car window, I could see tempting heaps of freshly fried *moong bhajias* piled up in neat pyramids. It was a local delicacy, served with very sweet, hot tea. After a welcome tea break we started off towards the Mahesh Khan estate, where cottages were booked for a night's stay. The sun had turned up its fierce heat—even though we were several miles above the sea level, we could melt. It was on one such hot summer noon at the Tulsi lake location when Dilip Kumar rephrased the *Suhana safar* lyrics humming, *suhana safar aur yeh mausam garam!*

Everyone chortled with delight hearing the Dilip Kumar version of the famous Mukesh song from *Madhumati*. At the narrow entrance into the Mahesh Khan Estate resort, we were greeted by a sturdy lock and unwelcome sign: No entry without permission. Deep wasted no time to chuckle:

'*Yeh to* Madhumati *wali baat hui na*! Do not enter without permission! *Yaad hoga aapko didi woh scene jahaan Dilip Kumar boldly cross karte hai aisi hi ek sign?*'

(This is exactly like that scene in *Madhumati*, you remember, when Dilip Kumar crosses over into the forbidden territory).

His words became a standing joke. Every time we had to cross the barrier the sign. 'No entry without permission' delayed us till the caretaker emerged from the woods to release us.

Waiting to be released, I noticed with a thrill, the landscape had marvelously changed around us. We passed through acres and acres of sky scraping pine trees. A nameless bird incessantly called. It sounded as if the bird was asking: *ka phal paako* (which fruit has ripened)? I never found out the bird's name except the colloquial one. But it was the same familiar bird call you hear in *Madhumati's* sound track and perhaps these were the same pine needles that crunched under Anand's feet on his way to the secret trysts with Madhumati. In that enchanting location, I had an uncanny feeling—as if I had walked right into the film. Nothing seemed to have changed in 55 years; the serenity of the hills, the endless pine woods, and the bird call piercing the dense silence was an overwhelming experience. It was surreal.

We soon settled into our individual cottages in the secluded Mahesh Khan, far away from the main residential neighbourhood of Bhowali. Finding me alone, true to his ilk, Deep wanted to interview me about *Madhumati*. He had, I realized, his own little agenda, to write a special feature on *Madhumati* and me. Reluctant at first, I decided to give in to his sincere request. Surrounded by sounds and images that reminded me again and again of *Madhumati*, I began to unwind, share intimate details about the film, people behind the scenes, specially its technical crew. I told Deep, for example, how the two *Madhumati* technicians, editor Das and his assistant Sakharam, had surprised me with the incredible story why the film was not allowed to celebrate its silver jubilee!

Madhumati, both editors had confirmed, was running house full from the very first week. The film completed twenty-four weeks in Bombay's Roxy cinema (the theatre no longer survives) opposite the Opera House. Incidentally, after *Madhumati, Sujata* was released at the Opera House—a well-known piece of vintage architecture. Whenever a film completes 25 weeks, the occasion is celebrated with tremendous fanfare. Unceremoniously withdrawn despite houseful, *Madhumati*, did not celebrate silver jubilee. The reason for this astounded me. According to editor Das:

> '*Madhumati* was first released in Calcutta; followed by its Bombay release on 19 September 1958. There were 18 or 20 prints released all over India. The film was an instant hit—super hit in fact. Salilda's music was the film's biggest attraction. But *Madhumati* was not allowed to celebrate a silver jubilee. It would have easily completed 25 weeks at the Roxy Cinema. There was a rule those days according to which Cinema owners had to give a huge bonus on the completion of 25 weeks to the cinema hall staff. They decided to withdraw the film from the theatre after 24 weeks to avoid paying bonus to its staff.'

Assistant editor Sakharam was more fortunate than the film. He received a hefty bonus for *Madhumati*. The very next year he got another bonus for *Sujata* which celebrated its silver jubilee in the Opera house: 'My salary was two hundred rupees. I received twelve hundred rupees as bonus—it was full six months' pay.'

It was Sakharam who opened my eyes to the unknown individual named Das Dhaimade. Both of them had many stories to share about BRP. But what interested me more at that point of time was that they knew many details about the making of *Madhumati*.

'Who is this Sakharam?' asked Deep.

A pertinent question that merits a reply. In fact, no one had a more humble beginning in the BRP production team than Sakharam Borsay. The 22-year-old uneducated youth from Dhule District had been a houseboy for Editor Hrishikesh Mukherjee's large household. Sakharam, however, had no qualms

about the fact that he was a houseboy. On the contrary, he
fondly recalled his struggling days:

> 'For many years I worked at Hrishida's house. I had become
> like their family member. Mohan studios, where Hrishida
> edited films, was next door to their house. His mother
> encouraged me to go to the studio. She told him to teach
> me how to edit films so that I could assist him one day. And
> I assisted Hrishida edit the first film he directed, *Musafir*.'

It was sometime in 2008. I remember we were feverishly working
on the Golden Jubilee celebration of *Madhumati* being held in
Globus—the single screen theatre. Out of the blue, one morning,
Sakharam turned up. I knew him by appearance. Had seen him
hang outside Hrishikesh Mukherjee's seaside bungalow on Carter
Road. Years before that I would see him work as the director's
houseboy in Mukherjee's Andheri residence.

Whenever I paused to rest, looked up from the tiny verandah
where I sat with Deep, before me was a *Madhumati* frame. The
gently swaying tall pine trees overhead, a slice of blue sky in
between, and the incessant bird call of an unknown bird echoed
breaking the monotony of a long, lazy afternoon. What a surreal
ambience. It had an unreal, dreamlike quality. I asked Deep if
he knew the name of the bird. It is the bird which says '*ka phal
pako*', Deep explained. Listening to tales about Baba's former
technicians, Deep had become engrossed in their stories.

BREAKING NEWS

I returned to Sakharam's story. The man was going through a
lean period when he came to visit me. He was obviously in dire
financial need. And I in need of an editor who had the time,
rather the inclination, to check Beta tapes of Baba's work, I
explained to Deep. I was aware Sakharam was a film editor.
Seeing him at a loose end, I asked if he would take on the job. He

agreed without fuss. During our negotiation, he informed me of having worked for Bimal Roy Productions—particularly for *Madhumati*. His assurance made me more confident. Instead of giving Sakharam a few hundred rupees, I gave him work. This resolved both our immediate problems. The job required him to come over several times. A chatty man, Sakharam was full of startling anecdotes, especially about the early phase of his career, especially the BRP chapter. His constant chatter, a noisy distraction, would amuse me.

I was, however, skeptical about the veracity of his stories. To his advantage was the fact that he had kept in touch with the few members of the erstwhile BRP unit. This included Baba's assistant Debabrata Sen, whom I knew. The other was a gentleman named Das. The last name kept cropping up several times during his chat. Das was an unfamiliar name to me as I did not associate it with BRP. I thought I knew all those who worked for Baba. But Sakharam insisted that Das babu, as he called him, was a noted film industry editor.

'Have you heard of an editor named Das?' I asked Deep. He shook his head.

One day when Sakharam insisted that Das and *not* Hrishikesh Mukherjee had edited 60 per cent of *Madhumati*—I stared at him with disbelief. Seeing the incredulity on my face, Sakharam began to protest aloud. When excited, Sakharam spoke in two languages, Bangla and Hindi. He asserted the editing of *Madhumati* was handled by Das Dhaimade alone and that he had assisted Das.

> '*Didi, biswas karun* (trust me). What I am saying is the truth, in fact; a lot of the field work of the film was done by Das babu. Bimalda would come at lunch time to oversee everything and take over for the rest of the day. *Aapni Das babu ke jiggesh koroon na keno?* (Why don't you ask Das babu?)'

And so, Sakharam's insistence made me to call Das one morning. A triumphant smile had lit up his face. For me, more amazement was in store. 'Can you believe, Deep, after fifty years of *Madhumati*, I was speaking to the man who had been a technician with my father since BT's *Maa* was made in 1951/2. Imagine being so ignorant of his existence!'

This is another classic case of invisibility! For an outsider like Deep, it was breaking news. Everyone believed Hrishikesh Muhkherjee had edited Bimal Roy's *Madhumati*. He was even awarded the Filmfare Trophy in 1958 for Best editing. I could hear the gentle whir of Deep's small recorder; it was busy listening to these stories, taking down surprising details.

Then, I was actually on my way to Das's apartment in Gamdevi. On the way, I tried to imagine people from Baba's film unit. But I could not recollect Das. His memory slipped away. The growing suspense had made me impatient to find out more on this mysterious elder editor. When I reached Das's apartment in an old block of their humble abode, the Dhaimade couple took me by surprise. They presented a picture of middle class respectability. In the twilight of his life, the discreet Das could even pass off as a retired small town school teacher. He did not look like the editor of famous films. He seemed a misfit in this aggressive, glitzy, celluloid world. 'The name Das is actually a nickname, he told me, Deep.'

His real name is Gurudas Dhaimade. Working with Bengalis in Bimal Roy's unit, Gurudas from Panjim, Goa, got nicknamed Das. He started as a humble assistant editor in the Bombay Talkies film *Maa*. Next he edited Ashok Kumar Productions' *Parineeta*. By the time Baba made *Naukri* and other films, he had been elevated to associate editor. In *Madhumati* too, his credit reads as the associate editor, not editor. Hrishikesh Mukherjee's name appears as the editor of the film. *Madhumati* gave Das full autonomy, as if by default. For him, *Madhumati* is the defining film of his long illustrious career. The fact his name did not appear as the 'editor' rankles him even after 55 years. Das shared the story of how he took charge of editing *Madhumati*:

> 'Work began for *Madhumati* after Dada's *Yahudi*. The editing was in full swing. By this time Hrishida became a director himself with his film, *Musafir*. Naturally I was going to edit his film. Because of the extra work, things were a bit messy while editing *Madhumati*. *Madhumati* and *Musafir* were edited simultaneously. There was a crunch of staff and time. With me were two assistants, Misra and one more, who edited movies which Bimalda made for outside producers. Bimalda asked one of them, who was assisting to edit *Madhumati*, what was happening in the edit room? He was told that Das is editing *Musafir*. I got a call saying that Bimalda wants to meet me. This was the first time I stepped into the BRP office! Dada scolded me saying that I was doing outside work. I argued that I am not doing outside work but working in the studio! I was too upset by then. I left Bimalda and returned the editing room keys.'

The confrontation made Das decide to quit Bimal Roy Productions that very day. When he received a second call from his director, it made him reconsider the hasty decision.

> 'After an hour I received another phone call. It was Bimalda again. He said, Das, complete the movie for me. I assured him then and there. I promised to complete the movie at the earliest. It took me full two months of day and night to edit *Madhumati*. The film's premier was fixed. This added to our pressure. Sakharam was of great help at this stage.'

Das continued the saga of editing *Madhumati* with quaint anecdotes thrown into the narrative and I was repeating the same to the one man audience, Deep Bhatt, sitting in the pine forest of Mahesh Khan on 26 June 2012:

'One evening Bimalda came to the editing room. We had ordered patties from a hotel nearby. Nobody had the guts to offer Dada any snacks. But somebody had to ask, he was in the editing room! Summoning up all the courage possible, I managed to ask if he would like to eat patties. He replied he would. When he came after 5 days, Dada asked, "Das where are the patties?" I said Dada, we don't eat patties everyday but if you want, we will order. By then the work was in place which made him extremely happy.'

Curious about the many challenges the editor faced during his work, I asked Das which was the most difficult part to edit in *Madhumati*. His reply was spontaneous:

'It was the film's climax. The climax was very difficult because of the effects and music tracks. If you remember that part in the beginning where the curtain is moving? That caused us terrible headaches as well. There were six tracks to be edited. Bimalda said that the curtain scene was exaggerated a little too much. He asked us to take the transcript and shorten that curtain effect. Rao of Raoko used to handle the Optical at the time. We did what was required of us. Bimalda was still not satisfied. On the sixth day he seemed pleased with our work. He was a very particular man. A perfectionist I must add. This was the difference between Bimalda and other directors. Hrishida had a chalta hai attitude. But not Bimalda. You see that in his films.'

CREDIT SNATCHING

The 1958 Filmfare awards was about to take place in the meantime. Film Technicians were asked to fill forms through their respective associations. That year, Das had edited two films, *Yahudi* and *Madhumati*. The editor's association called for an expert to make the final choice. The expert saw both films and his verdict went in favour of *Madhumati* for best editing. Das had edited more than 60 per cent of *Madhumati*, but it was his guru who went up the stage to get the Best Editor trophy. Das felt justifiably aggrieved. He laments even now about the episode:

> 'Not once did Hrishida ask me to collect the Filmfare Trophy. Instead he went on stage himself to take it! I agree Hrishida used to come to the BRP editing room and find out if things were in place. We always teased him, "Hrishida we are doing the actual work but at the time of the award, you will go to take it!" He denied he wanted awards and that is exactly what he did. This is one thing I am upset with Bimalda. He could have at least mentioned my name along with Hrishida as editor. I didn't want the award. I would have been overwhelmed thinking I had managed to satisfactorily edit a Bimal Roy film.
>
> Frankly, I have not seen a film like *Madhumati* till today. I would have been happy had he included my name. My name appears merely as assistant editor. Whatever the case, it proves we technicians have no authority whatsoever.'

I shared this lamentable tale with Deep. Talked about credit grabbing, the name of an old game played in the Indian film industry. He nodded in mute sympathy. Perhaps he too had some taste of the same game.

Grabbing credit for work one has not done has been a common film industry practice. It defies all logic but frequently rears its ugly head. Despite the fact there are trade associations to deal with disputed credits. Another serious issue before most associations is non payment of dues. In the Indian film industry, no one signs contracts. Most of the negotiations are by word of mouth, by trust. Where are safety nets in such hazardous deals when everything works on faith!

By temperament, Das was a timid man. He was far too decent to consider challenging a towering personality like Hrishikesh Mukherjee through his association. But he nurses a gnawing pain—of being side stepped for a film like *Madhumati*. Das may not possess the charisma, the personality of his guru, but there is no denying his enormous contribution to *Madhumati*. In fact Das contributed to several landmark films—he edited enduring classics like *Ganga Jamuna*, *Guddi*, *Anuradha* and *Abhimaan* to name a handful. When the 2010 Jury selected Das Dhaimade for the Bimal Roy Memorial's veteran category in creating these magnificent works, it was justice delayed. Das was overwhelmed by this gesture. Cherishing the Bimal Roy trophy we gave him in 2010, Das phoned to say: 'This is the best award for me. I remembered Dada and my days of working with him.'

Incredulous after hearing me talk of these incidents, Deep had asked: '*Kya aap yeh baateein likhengi apni kitaab mein?*' (Would you write all this in your book?)

'*Zaroor likhungi. Yehi to hai is kitaab ki khubi.*' (Certainly I shall write all this—this is the highpoint of my book), I answered him.

FORGOTTEN FIGURES FROM A DISTANT ERA

I remember there were two sound engineers who worked in BRP. The names are, Essa M. Suratwala and Dinshaw Billimoria. Essabhai's name, however, does not feature as an audiographer in the *Madhumati* booklet. But I remember Debu Sen confirming Essabhai was in charge of the sound recording. Little is known, less available on these two important industry technicians from the 1950s era. Unable to find anything substantial on the Internet about these veteran sound technicians, I concluded they have been consigned to darkness with many other technicians from the era. Had they worked today, they would be called sound designers.

From my brief visits to the studio, I recall the invisible Essabhai patiently recording somewhere in the deep bowels of the sound van. After a shot was taken all one heard was a faint 'sound OK' from a man one hardly saw. If he emerged from his position, a gentle smile, a calm visage greeted us. The last I remember of Essabhai was at Sunil Dutt's Pali Hill Preview theatre, Ajanta. I was holding a private show at the theatre. He came out from the projection room to greet me. Surprised I asked, 'Uncle, you here?' 'Beta, this is where I currently work,' he smiled. That was the last glimpse I had of Essabhai.

Surprisingly, art director Sudhendu Roy[1] too seems to have vanished without trace. I consider this surprising since Sudhendu Roy's daughter, Sharmistha Roy, is the gen-next celebrity. She has inherited her father's talent and established herself as a notable Bollywood art director working with Yashraj Films and other big Production companies. During the early phase of his professional career, Sudhendu Roy wore two hats in BRP. He was both the art director and costume designer. Most film credits of BRP bear his by-line in these two departments. In *Madhumati*, he styled all the costumes, with the exception of heroine Vyjayanthimala's wardrobe.

Someone informed me that Sudhendu Roy has been rated as one of the top ten art directors in the world on an Internet site. Not just in the domestic circuit but globally. I felt a colossal satisfaction hearing this. Sudhin kaka was a shy, moody man; he had in fact an air of the disheveled painter.

'Deep, did I say he wore two hats? I was wrong. He actually wore three hats. He was a film director as well. You may remember his first film that was made in 1971—*Uphaar*, based on a Tagore story. Earlier Satyajit Ray had made it as *Samapti*. However, it is as ace art director people remember the name of Sudhendu Roy.'

Rajinder Singh Bedi[2], the progressive Urdu writer, playwright and film director, wrote the dialogues for *Madhumati*. He was not on the production payroll but engaged to write the dialogues of the film. Previously, he wrote the dialogues of *Devdas*.

Madhumati continues to throw up dollops of surprises. Compared to other Bimal Roy films it has more dance sequences and an unbelievable eleven songs. And it won 11 Filmfare awards, practically in every category. This was an unbeatable record for many years. Amongst the dance choreographers appear three names—the name of Sohanlal appears first. Followed by the name of Sachin Shankar, a handsome dancer renowned for his artistic ballets, and lastly appears the name of Saytanarayan.

And next time you watch *Madhumati*, look carefully in the female chorus faces of the robust number *Daiya re daiya chadh gayo paapi bichua*—you may suddenly see the dancing queen, Saroj Khan on the screen. The lady was hardly thirteen at the time but danced like a diva. In a recent documentary film on Saroj Khan, Vyjayanthimala reminisced about the young Saroj who displayed tremendous virtuosity as a nameless wonder at the early age of thirteen. I believe her dance master Sohanlal married her—but their union was unhappy and short-lived.

THE DESSERT!

Dilip kaka—cinematographer Dilip Gupta[3]—was the veritable dessert amongst father's technical crew. As children, one of our greatest attractions in Bombay was spending time with Dilip kaka's family. Their tiny Matunga flat on tree lined College Road had many celebrated neighbours—Prithviraj Kapoor, the school boy Shashi, and the legendary K.L. Saigal. Manna Dey, the singing legend, came later to stay there.

In this land of glitz and glamour—Baba and Dilip kaka were like babes in the wood. They were closer than siblings. Left on their own, they spoke in the East Bengali dialect. Work or no work, the two were abundantly comfortable together. No social event in our home was complete without the Gupta family. In one of his interviews, Dilip kaka spoke emotionally about their friendship. Truly deep, it was a rare friendship: 'I had close professional relations with Bimal Roy. Bimal valued my suggestions. During any location, we stayed in one room. We used to discuss and discuss and discuss the film when we were not shooting. So while working, our heads would function as one.'

Dilip kaka started out as a bit actor in the New Theatres studios. Cast as the second male lead role in the forgotten film titled *Chorkanta*, he was offered the lead role in the next production which he declined—wisely. By then he had discovered a keen interest in cinematography. The following paragraph will give readers a detailed profile of this dynamic cinematographer.

'Dilip Gupta was the first Indian cinematographer to receive formal training in the discipline from Hollywood. And it certainly showed in the quality of this art [sic]. He attended the New York Institute of Photography and then worked briefly in Hollywood with the Paramount Studios. He worked with many of the great names of Hollywood including Walt Disney, Greta Garbo, Clark Gable, Douglas Fairbanks and others. He even trained in animation techniques in Walt Disney's Studios. On his departure from the US, Disney sketched him a goodbye card featuring the Three Little Pigs, Mickey Mouse and Goofy in his own hand. On his return to India, he rejoined the New Theatres despite an offer from the Bombay Talkies. He went on to work with famous Bengali directors like Pramathesh Barua, Nitin Bose, Phani Mazumdar and Charu Roy. He shot films featuring outstanding legends—K.L. Saigal, Pahari Sanyal, Kanan Bala and Leela Desai among others, forging life-long personal relationships with thse stars. He moved

to Mumbai in early 1942 to work with Sohrab Modi and
Acharya P.K. Atre. The films he worked on during this
phase were both Hindi and Marathi including *Dil ki baat,
Parinda* and *Maruchi Mausi…*'

Dilip kaka's body of work can be divided into two chapters. His
work with the New Theatres' directors, P.C. Barua, Nitin Bose
and Bimal Roy. In the second phase belong frothy, mainstream
type films with Sasadhar Mukherjee and Nasir Hussain. These
partnerships resulted in exquisite B&W cinematography with
notable films like *Deedar, Madhumati, Biraj Bahu, Gotama The
Buddha, Dil Deke Dekho, Jab Pyar Kisise Hota Hai, Prem Patra,
Benazir,* and *Yahudi.*

Interestingly, Dilip kaka had shot *Ajit*—the first Indian film
to be made in Kodachrome. It was also the country's first colour
film after World War II, in 16mm format, which was blown up
to a 35mm film. Many unknown and candid nuggets about him
are documented in a recent book by his daughter Champa Roy.
She records a particularly amusing anecdote:

> 'In 1957, Dilip Gupta had signed up yet another film with
> the Bimal Roy banner—the very, very famous film,
> *Madhumati*. He and Bimal Roy put in their best efforts
> and it became one of the era's greatest films. About this
> time, Dilip's fifth daughter was born. He wanted to name
> the baby Madhumati. But his wife strongly objected to the
> name as the heroine of this film commits suicide by jumping
> from the terrace!'

Dilip Gupta's work continues to inspire students and thespians
alike. One of his former students, the Pune-based cinematographer
K.K. Jaisawal has noted:

> 'As students we were taught that back-light creates the
> third dimension in a frame. Dilip saheb used back-light so
> sparingly and minimally; and yet his frames had the feel of

the third dimension. His low-key lighting with rich black was another point which struck me. In *Madhumati*, the mysterious scenes in the haveli's interior, Ugranarayan's (Pran) introduction when he comes in from darkness to light, the scene shot at the temple when Anand sees a group of people going to a fair in the night, are some of the features that haunted me in my dreams. *Madhumati* stands as a textbook film for students of cinematography.'

A celebrity endorsement from thespian Dilip Kumar, who shares his name and temperament, neatly sums up the distinguished cinematographer's position in the Bombay film industry.

'Dilip Gupta was the cameraman of three interesting films I did. Director Nitin Bose held him in high regard for his expertise and creativity. He was sincere, dedicated and respected the director's vision. His sense of lighting was so good that he created wonders with his camera. He showed how to break up the light and create movement of a train inside the compartment. He picturised yesteryear's film star Vanmala singing in a moving train. So realistic was this that Sohrab Modi of Minerva Films wanted to sign him. Techniques were not as advanced as today, so it was a wonder when Dilip Gupta created the effect of light breaking up when a fast moving train went by, simply using light and shadows.

It was during *Madhumati* that his expertise truly came to the fore. He won deserving critical acclaim for his evocative camera-work in *Madhumati* and I was happy to note that his imaginative photography, especially his skill in manipulating the lighting to create the desired illusion, came up for praise recently.'

Dilip kaka passed away at the age of 88, on 16 October 1999. He worked in the industry for five decades with several famous directors. Widely recognized as a pioneer with awards and citations, he received the President's Award for the documentary *Gotama The Buddha.*[4]

The first Bimal Roy Memorial Lifetime Award, 1997, for contribution to the film industry was conferred on this master of light and shade.

Deep Bhatt took down the information I had collected for the *Madhumati* book. It was a price I paid for his enthusiasm to accompany me on the journey. If I was on Madhumati's footsteps, Deep was on mine. Before I began my research, Deep had taken pains to visit Bhimtaal and Bhowali on his own, affirming places where Baba shot the film. He even took a photographer to document likely locations of crumbling estates and forests, some of which we visited the very first evening. Deep was confident the Bhawali sanatorium had been used as Ugranarayan's haveli. A claim that I could neither dismiss nor confirm. All the while we chatted, or texted, while collecting bits of information—there was some amount of substance. In his enthusiasm, every now and then this intrepid man would come up with new discoveries. He told me about the incredible Shankar Radios story—where Baba had taken his sound recording machine to be repaired. The story is a saga in itself.

I remember once Deep called up late, excited, to say that he came across a young girl who came running to meet him hearing the mention of *Madhumati*! The girl told Deep her grandmother had played Vyjayanthimala's double. But when the girl vanished without trace, I lost her story until it returned to me via Raj Shekhar Pant of Nainital and has been included in chapter VI.

NOTES

[1]Sudhendu Roy's second film *Saudagar* (1973) with Nutan and Amitabh Bachchan came two years later. It was based on the remarkably bold Bangla story titled *Ros* by renowned author Narendra Mitra. Produced by Rajshri Productions, these two films form a neat body of niche cinema that bears his lineage, his individual style.

[2]Rajinder Singh Bedi (1915–1984), considered one of the greatest twentieth century progressive writers of Urdu fiction, is the second most prominent Urdu fiction writer after Saadat Hasan Manto. Like Manto, he is known for his Partition tales. His writing was known for its sensitivity and earthiness. The novella *Ek Chadar Maili Si* was made into a Pakistani film first, *Mutthi Bhar Chawal* (1978), later in India as *Ek Chadar Maili Si* (1986), is a rare distinction for an Indian author to have his work on both sides of the border. As a dialogue writer, he wrote Hrishkesh Mukherjee's films *Abhimaan*, *Anupama* and *Satyakam*, and Bimal Roy's *Madhumati*. Bedi directed *Dastak* (1970), starring Sanjeev Kumar and Rehana Sultan and *Phagun* (1973), starring Dharmendra, Waheeda Rehman, Jaya Bhaduri and Vijay Arora.

[3]Details about Dilip Gupta have been taken from the book *A Portrait of Dilip Gupta: The Artist Who Painted with Light and Shade*, written and published by his daughter, Champa Roy 2010.

[4]*Gotama The Buddha* (1956): Received President's Gold Medal. The award winning documentary on the ancient teachings of Buddha also received a citation in Cannes for its moral beauty.

5

Dressing the Dream

I have yet to see one completely unspoiled star, except for the animals—like Lassie.

—Edith Head[1]

Our next destination was Ranikhet; and upon being told that the Bhowali market was a good place to find taxis, we headed in that direction on 27 June. It was sometime before Joshi found a suitable parking place on the precariously narrow bazaar road near the taxi stand. The plan was simple; find a suitable cabbie to drive us to Ranikhet that afternoon for a reasonable fee.

With all of us ready for the ubiquitous cup of chai, our delight knew no bounds when Joshi parked right opposite a tea-stall cum dhaba, adorned by the signboard, *Gud Chineez Cousins*—which we decoded correctly as 'Good Chinese Cuisine'. A quick look into the gloomy interior made us drop all desire for chai. None of us seemed to be brave enough to sample the 'Chineez Cousins'. We tripped across to the other side of the street in the hope of locating a less ambitious tea shop in the tightly knit commercial area. Around us open shops displayed fresh apricots, apples, and other exotic looking fruits. Unable to resist, I bought some for the forthcoming uphill journey.

An inexplicable feeling was overtaking me. As we drove through the steep hilly roads, or walked down the crowded Bhowali bazaar that noon, I kept looking over my shoulder for women dressed in flared ghagras and silver anklets or men with conical caps. It was foolish, I admit, but I seemed to be completely obsessed with looking for signs of a film made fifty-six years ago. *Madhumati* possessed me completely as I scanned the market place, its streets in the hope of finding someone or something answering that description. I was finally forced to concede that over the years, fashions and dress codes had changed dramatically. Specific cultural details that distinguish outsiders or tourists from locals were no longer in evidence.

Costumes of celluloid characters in film productions were critical in creating that dream-like quality evident on the silver-screen. Characters donning costumes differing from their real-life attire achieve several related objectives for everyone involved— from the director and costumer down to distributor and finally of course, the audience. I agree with Landis[2] that 'Costumes can't make a bad movie good, but they can make a good movie better'. The garb gives the dream a distinction, allowing the audience to live, albeit temporarily, in the director's dream or illusion.

Costumes set the stage of a film in two ways. Firstly, for the actors in a production: to give creative expression and bring a character more or less successfully to realization. Secondly, costumes enhance the locale of a story: in the way the use of props and sets create the illusion of realism for a discerning audience. During the black and white era, costuming did not eat into the film budget as it does in the contemporary context. Attention to detail was not always adhered to. An actor could get away with a bright purple top on an orange skirt as long as the style was suitable since the actual colours would not be visible. Razia Husain's memory proved to be important in this context. She remembers the exact colour of Dilip Kumar's attire

when she first spotted him playing the character Anand at the
outdoor location of *Madhumati* at Bhowali: 'I remember Dilip
Sahab was wearing an orange checked shirt and dark brown
pants...'

How fortunate that *Madhumati* was shot in black and white,
I laughed to myself, amused! The garish sartorial attire Razia
recalls would have knocked out all romance from the song *Dil
tadap tadap* or any similar romantic situation had the film been
in colour.

Meanwhile, Deep and his wife had found a place that served
hot tea with 'Chineez' pakoras. There seemed to be no getting
away from the 'Chineez' obsession! Leaving them to order, I
took a short walk for a last look at the quaint village shops. Joshi
was still busy with his mission of procuring a reliable driver. At
the peak of the tourist season, it was a tall order...

Given Baba's realistic cinematic vision, he must have studied
the local residents, their clothes and their habits when he selected
Bhowali as the *Madhumati* location. This diligence coupled with
his designer eye and traits, set him apart from other film directors
of the period—a point that has been consistently noted by film
academics besides his cast and crew. Always true to his beliefs,
he took great pains to match the milieu with the staging,
sometimes even intervening personally, to achieve the desired
effect, as we discovered. The dhotis of his peasant characters for
example, (particularly in *Do Bigha Zamin*) were left soaking in
tea all night to catch a light brown stain. The bleach would have
gone by next day and in a black and white film a dhoti dyed in tea
would reflect a suitably drab appearance. An effective ploy to
distinguish between the upper classes and the working class
characters that worked perfectly in Baba's films. In Hollywood
they have ageing specialists to effectively 'age' costumes for a
film. But in India, during that early period, it was a hands-on job
left to people like Kishan Dhamani and the BRP dressmen.

It was Raj Shekhar Pant who shared the eloquent memories of his father, Shri Pant:

> '...decked in their traditional attire and silver ornaments, the ladies would walk to the location negotiating a distance of six to eight miles on foot to the shooting spot along the stretch of the then kuccha road connecting Ghorakhal with the main Bhowali-Bhimtal road. A larger part of the song *Suhana safar* was shot exactly at the spot from where the trail ascends to the Ghorakhal Temple. Overlooking the temple was the summer villa of the Nawab of Rampur.'

Learning about the processes that went in to create the iconic impact which *Madhumati* still has, was enlightening. I could see for myself the perfectionist that was Baba. But contrary to the brusque, stand-offish manner one would expect from perfectionists, he was completely the opposite. The following anecdotes serve to tie up the importance the director gave to costumes in his cinema; and the position of importance he held his costumers in.

AUTHENTICITY AND ATTENTION TO DETAIL

It is common knowledge that authenticity mattered a great deal to a director of my father's reputation and temperament. Clare Wilkinson Weber's[3] question, 'Where in India can one find tribal people who look quite like this?' is best answered by the authentication of the individuals I spoke to during the course of writing this book. They confirmed that Baba used people from the villages as junior artistes in the chorus or the village fair sequences. To represent local colour and imbue authentic flavour, the makeshift actors were not given costumes, but briefed to wear their own personal outfits. Raj Shekhar Pant, a lecturer of English at Nainital shared how villagers from distant rural areas turned up in droves to watch the shooting. Women dressed in all their finery would arrive, simply to watch the magic of capturing action into a black box. One must remember that at the time *Madhumati* was being filmed, not many villagers had witnessed a film shooting. This gregarious lecturer as well as many others confirm how a local woman, found to resemble Vyjayanthimala was made to stand-in for the famous southern star. The poor unsuspecting woman was made to run downhill several times and even enact tricky parts that required physical agility. All this was done, ostensibly to spare the actress of course. This was confirmed by an elderly tea stall owner, Harish Chandra Arya in the Gethia region too. Raj Shekhar Pant observes:

> 'I met the septuagenarian Kamla at Nainital. She remembers seeing Dilip Kumar strolling on the lawns of the bungalow and out of curiosity she and her friend Geeta Sah went to see them. It was then that they were asked by Bimal Roy and Dilip Kumar about the need for local co-operation. Quite a few of her friends, mostly Sah families of Bhowali and Nainital thus got an opportunity to work as junior artistes in the film. She was part of the song *Julmi sang aankh ladi.* And in the song *Suhana safar,* she was amongst the women carrying pitchers. Kamla recalled a Bombay choreographer teaching them the steps and spending days rehearsing.'

In *Madhumati,* specifically, the need to locate the story in its correct cultural setting was felt strongly enough for a local dress-man and tailor to be employed. On my journey to the actual film location, I traced people who shed some light on how costume details and local flavour were infused in this film. The film centres around a hill-side community, little known to wider India at the time. I took for granted that some artistic license would have been embellished into the various characters' costumes. I did not expect to find that cultural context and social realism had played so vital a part in recreating a tiny, charming township set high in the Kumaon hills in sharp contrast to Hindi cinema of today, where tribal characters (usually used in song-and-dance numbers) wear outlandish and unrealistic costumes. *Madhumati* took a different stance. Whether it was the costume of the haughty landlord, the lowly servant or the estate manager, the clothes depicted throughout the film document the social history of the era. But what of the outfits of the leading lady—did they ring true to the ensemble of the local Kumaoni women? I was anxious to discover the answer. Did the diva-esque heroine over-rule her director in order to wear a more 'fetching and fashionable' outfit?

The iconic Hollywood costume creator Edith Head once remarked: 'You can lead a horse to water and you can even make it drink, but you can't make actresses wear what they don't want to wear.'

Did Vyjayanthimala create fashion anew for herself? She certainly did, with the help of her grandmother Yadugiri Devi who is part of the film's credits. The Gethia tea-stall owner, Harish Chandra Arya, confirmed that women in the Pithoragarh district still dress in the manner depicted in *Madhumati*, sporting the *soota* (a marriage symbol), around their neck and flouncy, layered ghagras.

It may be argued that Baba's films did not require designers like Bhanu Athaya, Manish Malhotra or Tarun Tahiliani as his stories epitomized the daily struggles of the underprivileged, ordinary people, peasants, jobless young men, the girl-next-door, dalit women, middle class housewives—Indians whose social aspirations did not include high-end designer outfits. Clare Wilkinson-Weber has been researching on costumes in Hindi cinema and she commented[4]:

'Films—whether Roy's or anyone else's—are not generally about costume, it is true. But costume lays a foundation for the audience's sense of what is going on. It guides them towards complex and layered conclusions. An anecdote relayed to me by Kamini Kaushal from her experience of filming *Biraj Bahu* (1954) confirms that Bimal Roy understood this well. As her character falls deeper into the chasm of poverty and isolation, her saree becomes thinner and more ragged. For forty days, she told me, she wore the one saree her character was supposed to own.

When they were not filming, Roy himself would shred the saree to break it down and age it. In this case, and maybe others undocumented, we learn that not only was Roy a hands-on director, but that he cared enough about how the costumes looked to intervene directly in ensuring they produced the look that he wanted.'

Old working stills confirm what Clare has documented. Some of those faded images show Baba shredding sarees with infinite patience even as his actors rehearsed. To ensure the right effect, he took on jobs that could have been done by assistants. I remember a coarse black cotton striped saree that was specially imported from a village fair in West Bengal for Sadhana's costume in *Parakh* (1960). I managed to procure one of these black cotton sarees for my own college-girl wardrobe surreptitiously when my mother's gaze was averted (it costed the princely sum of eight rupees in old money). That simple black handloom saree with thin red and white stripes became something of a fashion statement, setting a trend among our Sophia College circle. Many of my classmates thought it extremely chic.

From the outset, I had observed the authenticity of the costumes designed for *Madhumati*. And during the course of our trip to the Ranikhet and Almora region I spoke to a few local friends, seeking their opinion about this issue. Did they represent the region? Indeed, were these outfits representative at all? Did the costumes seem 'real'?

I was heartened when Deep Bhatt, who belongs to that region, confirmed that Madhu's clothes in *Madhumati*, were considered authentic Kumaoni. The flouncy ghegria or Indian skirt she wears, for example , made in multiple layers is still worn by women in the interiors while the thick, silver choker that was around Madhu's neck is also an ornament that hill women wear. Deep pointed out that Charan Das's (Johnny Walker) attire was so authentic, particularly his conical cap, that he could have easily passed off as a local.

MAKING MADHUMATI MATCH THE MILIEU

Post-independence was not an easy time for film-making in the country. And though one would have thought that borders between communities and places and people would by this stage be unimportant, the north-south divide in India remains a cultural reality. It has not always been easy for those achieving a degree of success in one region to make the crossover into the other camp, regardless of the language barrier. Typically the Hindi film industry is a difficult place to make a mark in. But talent finds a way, as it did in 1951 when a sensational danseuse from South India made her debut in *Bahar*[5]—a remake of the Tamil film *Vazhkai* (1949). Her extraordinary footwork and radiant beauty made Hindi film-going audiences sit up and take notice. Vyjayanthimala had just begun her career, with two regional language films to her credit—the Telegu *Jeevitam* (1950), and *Vazkai* in her mother tongue Tamil. With the release of *Bahar*, the refreshingly young Vyjayanthimala proved herself a competent cross-over actress from the south to the north. Single-handedly she paved a career path for other sensational actors from the south who followed her footsteps to conquer the Hindi film industry, notably Rekha, Hema Malini and Sridevi.

Vyjayanthimala's memorable dance number to the song *Nandagopala* was an instant craze. Critic Maithili Rao giggled as she recalled how little girls were made to imitate this complicated dance routine before the standard captive audience—dinner guests. Before the current craze of the mother-in-law v/s daughter-in-law feuds on the small screen, or the popularity of KBC, dinner party entertainment was to the domain of talented children. The entire family watched with bated breath, lest the little feet miss a vital step and mess up the moves. Maithili Rao added:

> 'Like the song *Chammak Challo*, *Nandagopala* was an absolute rage. And Vyjayanthimala's panelled lehnga became a fashion statement of the time. Copied by eager teenagers who wanted to look cool, my elder sister stitched one for me in green and yellow panels and I enjoyed its lush feel for a long time.'

Vyjayanthimala enjoyed a great advantage in the costume department in the form of an in-house seamstress—her grandmother Yadugiri Devi who created innovative garments to suit her granddaughter's fashion needs. Later this included custom-made garments for her numerous film roles. All this went a long way in cementing her position as a star on the rise from the southern to the northern Indian silver-screen skies.

BRP had no designated costume designer for *Madhumati*; or any of the other productions for that matter. Dilip Kumar had his own preferred menswear store, but a competent tailor with the production company would also rise to the occasion. I was right in assuming that Vyjayanthimala's costumes were custom-made for her by Yadugiri Devi, though Vyjayanthimala remembers that they were discussed in great detail with art director Sudhendu Roy, in charge of art direction and the general costumes of the film. He made sketches of the outfits; dressman Kishan Damania accomplished the job.

'Costumes for me in *Madhumati* were done by my grandmother. She consulted a book on Indian folk costumes. The costumes were stitched in Mumbai by the Bimal Roy Production tailors and dress men. The fabric was bought locally from Handloom House. As the location of the shooting was in a cold place like Nainital, thick, warm material was used for some of the costumes. It was a black and white film; restrictions were placed on the fabric colour. We could have only maroon, brown, and beige and sometimes blue. The jewellery I wore came from my private collection of silver. I like silver and had a good collection. We chose what looked authentic. Finally, it was what the director wanted—how he wished me to appear, that mattered most. I had to look rustic as well as innocent... this was the brief I followed for my costumes for *Madhumati*.'

This is how the actress looked at ease in her ordinary village girl garb. Making not only a mark on the memory of audiences for the moment during the screening of the film, but by creating a fashion statement long after the film had been forgotten. Today, modern department stores capitalize on this sort of popularity by creating clone costumes based on item-numbers for little girls. Disney Princess outfits are probably the western equivalent to this phenomenon of film fashion seeping into popular fashion culture. Mainstream Hindi cinema has often created spectacular wedding outfits, faithfully copied by brides-to-be across the nation. The Indian diaspora has always been particularly partial to Bollywood inspired couture.

Madhumati was a precursor in influencing fashion tastes of a more innocent time. And, I do not think I am overstating the romanticism of the period. As a film, *Madhumati* falls squarely into the Romantic Era of 1950s Hindi cinema.

CREATING COSTUMES AND CREATING CHARACTERS

Dressmen and dresswalas were great assets of production houses in the 1950s when BRP was at its peak. This explains the emergence of Maganlal and Chhotubhai dresswalas. At this point, dressmen should be distinguished from dresswalas. The work of the dressmen was to maintain costumes on the set. Most dressmen came from tailoring backgrounds and would work with the company tailor, or knew all the tailors capable of fabricating the costumes required. Some, like the Bimal Roy Productions' dressman Kishen Dhamani, possessed the dual advantage of being a cutter and a tailor. Clare Wilkinson-Weber continues:

> 'Dresswalas have always been important, I think, for films because of the scale of operations they have (Maganlal, Chhotubhai are the biggest, I think) and because they are used to making some of the more off-the-wall demands of films (for fantasy costumes, historical costumes etc). However, I think that the principals have usually got their work done elsewhere if they could. So female stars would have their preferred masters, and men would have their preferred menswear suppliers. For mundane demands, or a film like *Devdas*, my guess is that the art director would give directions; I don't actually know the details of how they got measurements or did fittings, which I ought to know, but it didn't come up in interviews. It may be the company tailor who did that. Dresswalas were also considered to be authorities regarding regional dress, as well as historical dress. Maganlal played a big role in a film like *Mughal-e-Azam*.'

Clare Wilkinson-Weber's understanding of the historical intricacies and social connotation of costumes worn in *Madhumati* simplifies my work:

'Dilip Kumar's character, Anand, in *Madhumati*, a film set in the Himalayan foothills, dressed in western style shirts and trousers, but no tie, a casual shoulder bag slung over his arm. Anand's costume distinguishes him not only from the tribal people, but also from the forest workers, the evil landlord and his henchmen, and even the picnickers he meets towards the film's end. He opts for a safari shirt and a cravat. In this regard, he is clearly unlike Devendra, whose narration starts off and concludes the film. That character, also played by Dilip Kumar, is as I said, thoroughly westernized. Madhavi is the double of Madhumati who agrees to help Anand avenge Madhumati's death. Both women are similar in their enjoyment of the nivi sari's touch of modern glamour, yet they are unlike in most other ways. That a costume may mask moral and social positions is a proposition that adds depth and interest to others among Roy's female characters. Vyjayanthimala is presented to best effect, alternating her roles of Madhu, the tribal heroine, and Madhavi, the modern woman and folk dancer, and later, Radha, the wife and mother who is glimpsed briefly at the conclusion of the film. As Madhu, she is dressed in a folk costume, but in typical filmi fashion, Vyjayanthimala's figure is flattered by the dress. And her face, of course, is beautifully set off by jewellery and make-up. There are several costume changes, although not so many by contemporary standards. The one important communicative element of her costume is its belt. The belt is part of the public "face" of the costume, an elemental component of its decency. Without it, Madhu is vulnerable, compromised. She is beltless when Ugranarayan attacks her, for example. *Madhumati* also has several dance sequences in which matched costumes feature. Some find these obviously contrived scenes amusing and baffling. Where in India can one find tribal people who look quite like this? But questions of authenticity and aesthetic

integrity seem somewhat out of place in what is, essentially,
a ghost story.'

This brings to mind what I heard from close friends about Dilip
Kumar's role model. The man he admired enough to follow his
sartorial tastes as well as hair styles—the suave Hiten Chaudhury,
Baba's good friend and an important film producer of the 1950s.
Hiten Chaudhury was Dilip Kumar's mentor for several years, a
fact unknown to many.

Baba's debut film *Udayer Pathe*[6] is an excellent reference
point on how costumes defined the cultural aspirations of its
characters. It also affirms Clare Wilkinson-Weber's statement
that Baba was particular about the look of his films. His concern
impacted the costumes the characters wore. Anup, the hero, for
example, is a struggling writer. He lives off ghost-writing for an
influential corporate executive. An ardent swadeshi, he takes
pride in sporting handspun Indian attire, never mind how torn
and tattered, and speaks chaste Bengali. His fierce pride does
not allow him to mix English and Bengali while conversing in
order to maintain the purity of the two languages. Anup's boss,
on the other hand, is presented in formal western attire; he
speaks English self-consciously. These features distinguish the
two men who become bitter political adversaries in the concluding
chapter of the film.

The costume changes in this film are dramatic—the director
uses them to signify the metamorphosis of the film's heroine
Gopa and charting the change in the crests and troughs of her
character. As the film begins, Gopa, who is introduced as the
classmate of the hero's sister Sumita, wears fine Dacca jamewar
sarees, advertising her elite class. As the narrative progresses,
Gopa is bitterly disillusioned with her own class; she begins to
dress down even as the intimacy between her and the writer-
hero grows. At one point she is clad in simple white khadi which
the hero appreciates.

The phenomenal popularity of *Udayer Pathe* made women of that era want to dress, talk and even walk like the heroine Gopa. What is so commonplace today, with life imitating filmy artistry, was unique in the 1940s and 50s. Suddenly the market was flush with replicas of the '*Udayer Pathe* necklace'. Binata Bose who played Gopa in the bilingual film, unintentionally created an iconic fashion trend to be followed by the bored, rich, upper class Bengali women of that time.

Interestingly, no screen credit is accorded to any particular fashion designer in *Udayer Pathe*. Film credits were not meticulously managed (though not very different, even today). Of course costume designing gathered an impressive following when the inimitable Bhanu Athaiya won the coveted Oscar for *Gandhi* (1983) but it is quite the norm for wives or daughters of well-known directors to be the unpaid and uncredited costume designers and art designers in the history of Indian cinema. One may safely assume that decisions regarding costumes were jointly taken by the art director and director of the film, as per the accepted practice.

Edith Head, the Grand Dame on this subject, hits the nail on the head when she says: 'What a costume designer does is a cross between magic and camouflage. We create the illusion of changing the actors into what they are not. We ask the public to believe that every time they see a performer on the screen he's become a different person.'

I do not think I am wrong in saying that my father's films have remained credible for the aspiring Indian middle class even though more than half a century has passed since they were made. The reason for this has as much to do with his selection of narratives, his nuanced treatment, as with the manner his characters behaved, and *appeared* in these films to render them credible. The costumes in his films added flair to the subject as film academics and audiences observed. *Madhumati* was given the social realist treatment in terms of its costumes, if not in terms of the storyline or setting. Dressing the dream somehow strengthens and enhances the dream-like quality of this film. Strangely this very quality also sets the timeless tone that *Madhumati* retains for new audiences, and accurate costuming is therefore part of a story well-spun.

My rumination about film costumes, fashion designers and about *Madhumati* was interrupted by the triumphant news that Joshi had found a driver named Narayan who would drive Maithili and me for two thousand rupees right up to our destination—Hotel West View, on Mall Road in Ranikhet. It sounded perfect!

'*Didi, lekin us gaadi mein AC nahi hai,*' Deep warned. I waved my hand negligently and said: '*Arrey chalega, Deep!*'

We got into Narayan's warm Wagon R. It was time to bid adieu to Joshi, Deep and his wife Hansi—they would drive down to Haldwani after we left. Little did I suspect as the taxi made its way uphill that Ranikhet would uncover more details about the *Madhumati* location from a most unlikely source.

NOTES

[1]Edith Head (1897–1981): Eight-time Academy Award winner. Most awards won by any woman costume designer, her films include *Rear Window* (1954), *The Sting* (1973) and *Sunset Boulevard* (1950).

[2]In her extensive introduction discussing the tradition, art and magic of costume design in Hollywood, Deborah Nadoolman Landis covers each decade, examining the history of design in each era. See for more detail and photographic imagery from Hollywood past and present in Landis, *Dressed: A Century of Hollywood Costume Design*, 1940s (2007: 133–177).

[3]See list of contributors.

[4]For further reading, Clare Wilkinson-Weber's essay: 'The Politics of Costumes in the Films of Bimal Roy' in *Bimal Roy: The Man Who Spoke in Pictures*, ed. Rinki Roy Bhattacharya.

[5]*Bahar* (1951), produced by AVM Productions. Starring: Vyjayanthimala, Karan Dewan, Pandari Bai, Pran, Omprakash and Leela Mishra. The film marked the debut of Vyjayanthimala.

[6]*Udayer Pathe* (1944): The first film to be written, directed and photographed by Bimal Roy, the bilingual film revolutionized Indian cinema.

6

On Madhumati's Footsteps

Suhana safar aur yeh mausam haseen, hamein dar hai hum kho na jayen kahin.

—Shailendra

ON MADHUMATI'S FOOTSTEPS

The road narrowed treacherously as the car wound its way uphill from Bhowali. It hugged the mountain wall on one side while the other side plunged deep into a thorny gorge. The Kosi River, also known as Kosila, was a parched riverbed in summer. We could see it running along like a thin silver ribbon at the bottom of the gorge. With each passing mile, the gorge grew deeper as we ascended towards Ranikhet. The steep mountain roads seemed to be broad enough for only one vehicle and I dreaded to think of what could happen if a second vehicle came along! Drivers of that region could pass driving tests anywhere with flying colours; I tried to comfort myself, training my thoughts to the Kainchi Dham dhaba my friend Mala had recommended for their rajma-chawal and delicious aloo parathas. The welcome vision of a piping-hot aloo paratha served to distract me momentarily from the car's drunken swerving on hairpin bends.

The greatest distraction, however, was in reliving that morning's incredible discoveries in Ghorakhal and at the Gethia Sanatorium. What an extraordinary slice of luck! A real life coincidence, as if scripted by Bollywood.

Our forays on the first day to the old bungalows in and around Mahesh Khan yielded nothing. To my frustration, I realized that none of them were *Madhumati* locations. In his enthusiasm, Deep Bhatt had assumed that the private residences in the vicinity of the Bhowali Sanatorium could have been the location for Ugranarayan's mansion. He claimed to have found a period armchair similar to the one in the *Madhumati* haveli. Critically analysing those dilapidated places, I was certain that the shooting could not have taken place in any of them. The rooms were far too small to manoeuvre the huge Mitchell camera normally used and I was convinced that Ugranarayan's mansion had been a sprawling studio set. A week later, Raj Shekhar's email confirmed this: 'Parts of the Rampur Nawab's residence were shown in the film as the residences of Pran and Dilip Kumar in the films [sic].'

I had followed Deep on this wild goose chase, confident that we would stumble onto something. I tried my best to match the film with places we saw—unfruitfully. By the final morning before we left for Ranikhet, a nagging suspicion that the trip could be completely unsuccessful was slowly unfurling at the back of my mind, when Taran's casual remark teased me. Ghorakhal—both Taran and Razia had insisted had been the location for the *Madhumati* shoot. I perked up once again; I had to visit Ghorakhal before we bid farewell to Bhowali.

After an early breakfast at the Mahesh Khan rest house, we got into Joshi's car with the intention of driving up the main Bhimtal-Bhowali road, in search of Ghorakhal. We reached a crossroad with a prominent sign post pointing in the direction of the Ghorakhal Sainik School. None of us could decide which

road to follow next. The place seemed unromantic, deserted at
that early hour. Perhaps we needed to toss a coin like Anand in
Madhumati, I remarked jocularly. A small tea stall manned by a
listless youth cleaning it seemed a likely place to garner
information. Sitting outside in the shade was an elderly man, his
face hidden by the paper he was reading. Parking the car opposite
the shop, Joshi shouted to the boy: '*Arre suno yaar, yaha koi film-
wilm ki shooting huyi thi kya? Yeh bahut purani film thi—naam hai
Madhumati?*' (Listen man; was any film shot around here? A
very old film—*Madhumati*?)

The boy continued with his business, ignoring us. I suggested
that we ask the man behind the newspaper. He belonged to an
earlier generation, more likely to remember an old film like
Madhumati. I stepped out of the car towards him and though he
lowered the newspaper on hearing me approach, he displayed a
complete lack of interest.

'*Namaste bhai-saab,*' I said in my best Hindi.

'I believe that a film called *Madhumati* had been shot in
Ghorakhal about fifty-six years ago? Would you know anything
about this?'

I had barely completed my sentence when he answered:
'*Haan huyi thi!*' (Yes, it had taken place here!) There was no
missing the aggressive undertone!

Rendered speechless by his admission, I almost lost my
balance, only to be steadied swiftly by the chivalrous Deep.
Introducing me as the daughter of the film's director he took
over, asking the man if we could talk to him about the film
shooting. The man stood up with a gloomy expression and
began to walk into the empty tea shop. Eagerly, we followed him
through the empty shop, lest he disappear through a small sparse
room, possibly his office that opened into a panoramic view of
the entire valley.

We perched on a bench like chirping canaries in a row, eager for information. The gentleman, a retired school teacher named Harish Chandra Arya, made no effort to hide his resentment at being deprived of his morning reading. Meanwhile we were jubilant; we had finally chanced upon an eyewitness and we attacked him with questions with gusto. I desperately hoped for a few authentic vignettes about the shooting which had taken place right across the street. Finally we elicited the following information:

> 'One afternoon, the fourteen-year old Harish Chandra Arya was on his way home from school but a huge crowd around the area where we were currently seated interrupted his journey. He was told that a film's shooting was taking place; all around people were hanging like bats from trees for a better view. That film, he remembers was *Madhumati*, but hailing from a conservative family, watching films was a taboo and consequently he had not seen the film. Oddly, his wife had seen it.'

Keen to establish the authenticity of the costumes worn in *Madhumati*, I ventured into new territory to ask Mr Arya if locals, especially women from the Kumaon hill region, dressed in a similar fashion. He conceded unenthusiastically that the ghagra worn by the film's heroine was common attire in the interiors, especially women from the Pithoragarh area. Maithili and Deep tried their hand at charming the man in vain. Deep remarked that the 'soota' or the silver necklace was also common amongst hill women. The ice steadfastly refused to melt, even though the barometer read 40 degrees in the shade!

In ten minutes we took leave of the inhospitable Harish Chandra Arya—I believe he would have thrown us out had we stayed any longer. But I consoled myself with the fact that he had unwittingly done us a big favour—he had identified the exact shooting spot. After leaving his tea shop (no tea drunk), we retraced our steps from the crossroad. It is truly abominable to dwell on the fact that none of us thought of proceeding on the road leading to the Ghorakhal Sainik School, a mere stone's throw away. '*Arey yaar, wohi to hai Rampur Nawab ka Estate House!* The place we spent most of our summers. Today the Nawab's former property houses the Ghorakhal Sainik School. *Madhumati* was shot just outside our place!'

Razia lamented, hearing that we did not visit the school which was the main location. Her email painted a charming picture about the momentous event of her life—the outdoor shooting of *Madhumati*:

> 'Next day the entire unit descended upon us—cars, vans, cameras et al. Our front lawn was full of people; the quiet Ghorakhal estate had suddenly come to life. Bimalda and Dilip Sahab arrived soon after. Bimalda looked pre-occupied—busy with cameras and shots. And oh Gawd! Dilip Sahab! So-oo handsome!! He was wearing an orange checked shirt and dark brown pants.
>
> Then the first shot was taken. It is the scene where Anand is looking over the hills. The music of the song *Suhana safar* starts in the background. Bimalda was strolling around our lawns. The huge house was on top of the hill with the mountain range around the estate. Bhimtal down below was being photographed. There he came over the clump of mountain lilies and waited to take a close up but the stones around were throwing too much glare on the cameras.
>
> Bimalda asked my father: "*Yahaan koi dhoti milegi?*"
>
> We looked at each other without understanding what a dhoti meant. Being conservative Muslims who wore sherwani and pyjamas, a dhoti was an unfamiliar apparel. Dilip Sahab came forward to explain, "*Bimalda ka matlab hai chaddar.*"

A bedsheet was promptly brought out and hung as a reflector frame for the first shot to be taken. Dilip Sahab is looking over the hill and the background music for the song *Suhana safar* starts. This can be seen in the song when he sings the line—*Yeh kaun hasta hai phoolon mein chupkar*. Father had organized lunch for the entire film unit. I was too young to remember how he organized the massive feast, summoning cooks, khansamas, murg and machli from Rampur overnight. I still wonder how he did it. But I do remember how much Dilip Sahab and Bimalda enjoyed the meal. Their fingers dripping with korma, everyone had complimented us that the food was "lajawab", out of this world.'

THE THIRD EYE

It was on 27 June that an invisible hand beckoned us beyond the Ghorakhal stretch to Gethia. We had no inkling of the treasures that Gethia had buried in its bosom when we arrived and asked for directions to the local sanatorium. All the while, my heart ached to hear someone, just anyone, say: 'Sure a film called *Madhumati* was shot here.'

Uncanny as it may sound, within a few seconds of arriving at the sanatorium, we were destined to hear those magic words. A small crowd of curious onlookers gathered around us as we asked if anyone knew about the shooting of a film. It was certainly a welcome change from the taciturn Mr Arya of Ghorakhal.

One of the guys pointed up where an elderly man squatted with his cronies on the steps of the sanatorium: '*Us aadmi ko malum hoga. Woh yahaan pachas saal se kaam kar raha hai.*' (That man ought to know. He has been working here for more than fifty years).

This information was accompanied by the enthusiastic approval of the onlookers and the elderly man was literally hauled down from his perch to the spot we stood. I invited him to sit under the shade of a tree as he introduced himself as Mangulal, the cleaner of the Gethia sanatorium for many years till his retirement. Unable to assess his exact age, I asked him; *Ab aapki umar kitni hogi Mangulalji?* (How old would you be now?)

He replied innocently: *Yehi kuch saath saal!* (Must be sixty something.)

The spectators burst into loud guffaws as a young man teased: *Chacha, aap to assi saal ke upar hain.* (Uncle, you must be well over eighty years.)

Mangulal chose to ignore this allegation; he was too engrossed in informing us that *Madhumati* had indeed been shot in a place called Chir Dhar, in the vicinity. When I asked if he was certain that the film was indeed *Madhumati,* he was clearly amused: *Arrey, wohi fillum na jisme Daalip Kumar they?* (Isn't it the film with Dilip Kumar?)

Mangulal was around twenty when his young eyes lit up with the excitement of watching a film shooting. His vivid memory includes the sight of the massive crowd attracted by the event. People came from far away, from other towns, he recalled with pride. They climbed every branch of the trees for vantage positions. No film had been shot in Gethia before or since, emphasized Mangulal. According to him, the shooting went on for a whole week. There were so many cars (a first for that area), and the food for the production unit came from a hotel. Mangulal's firsthand account, however sketchy, accurately established another location site of *Madhumati.* We stood on a piece of sacred ground. I was ready to kiss it with joy! Looking up at the ancient trees all around me, I imagined people hanging on their branches in excitement simply to watch Dilip Kumar sing *Dil tadap tadap* in the sylvan glade of Chir Dhar. Mangulal's words were confirmed ten days later by Raj Shekhar Pant's email in greater detail:

'During the course of the *Madhumati* location shooting,
the Bhowali-Ghorakhal area was the happening zone. A
few scenes were shot in a settlement midway between
Bhowali and Bhimtal in a place known as Mehragaon. One
song was shot at Gethia, close to the sanatorium. Some
shooting was done at Garampani—at the river bend that
flows along the roadside settlement.'

During the outdoor shooting of *Madhumati*, its stunning hero,
the dapper Dilip Kumar was in his late thirties and in excellent
physical form. He reminisced about enjoying the long outdoor
spell. For the entire *Madhumati* crew it was like an extended
picnic as the star recalled: 'I have always enjoyed outdoor work.
In *Madhumati* the outdoor work was to become the core of
the film and that idea alone filled me with the excitement of a
child who is promised a long vacation at a destination of his
choice.'

All this talk about locations reminded me of the time I
accompanied the film unit to Igatpuri. My experiences of a
single day seemed to pale in comparison to Mangulal's reminisces
of a week exposure to film shooting. He was the third eyewitness
now to the *Madhumati* outdoor shooting, following Razia and
Harish Chandra Arya.

From Debu Sen I heard other interesting tales of the time
when the location moved near Igatpuri. I asked him if it was true
that Dilip Kumar had problems giving dates during the outdoor
shooting of *Madhumati*. Were the dates clashing with the
shooting of his home production, *Ganga Jumna* for example?
Debu agreed that the shooting of both the films was taking place
at the same time in Igatpuri. 'Everyone from Dilip Kumar's unit
was staying on location. Even the dubbing of Vyjayanthimala for
Gunga Jumna was taking place on the Igatpuri location.'

Debu remembers the time when Dilip Kumar was required
to come for just a day from his Igatpuri location to shoot at

Mohan Studios. He reported half an hour before the appointed
time for the shooting of the very first scene in *Madhumati* when
Anand's past life brims to his consciousness. Baba had explained
the scene to his hero, but being a leisurely man, Baba was late by
an hour that day. To tease Baba, Dilip Kumar prepared a placard
with only two words: 'Welcome Bimalda'. My father glanced at
the placard, with a smile and disappeared into the bowels of
the set.

Debu continued his journey into the past:

'Yusuf-bhai had to rush back that evening. So by lunch
time, Bimalda managed to take ten shots. This was
remarkable by his standards. Bimalda had a reputation for
being extremely slow. While we were canning the eleventh
shot, assistant cameraman, Chuni Chatterjee let out a
shriek, "Bimalda! Oh!"

We thought Chuni had received an electric shock
or something terrible like that. It took some time for
Chuni to calm down. Then he confessed that he had
forgotten to open the shutter of the camera! This meant
that none of the last ten shots had been captured.
"A sheer waste," he said, though Bimalda did not utter a
single word of rebuke. In his cool style, Bimalda announced
a lunch-break and the unit moved to the big dining-room
on the first floor of Mohan Studios. At the lunch
table Yusuf-bhai complained to Bimalda with utmost
seriousness:

"If I was in your place Bimalda, I would sack the
cameraman and his assistant. Imagine, ten shots were not
taken." Looking at him calmly, Bimalda replied, "Yusuf,
imagine if this was discovered after packup—what would
have happened then?"

Rendered speechless, Dilip Kumar could only say:
"*Kamaal hain aap, Bimalda!*"

After the shooting, Dilip Kumar put a hand on Chuni's shoulder and said, "Chuni, I have a friend who is now a judge in the Allahabad Court. When we used to play football, he always shot an own-goal. Every time I meet him, I tease him about this. Chuni, when you become a famous cameraman, I will ask you—did you remember to open the shutter?"

And guess what? After lunch, ten shots were canned. A remarkable feat for Bimalda...'

The entire process of matching the outdoor hill station ambience with a studio environment during the making of *Madhumati* can constitute an entire chapter. Fortunately, the match was near perfect. The audiences never made out the difference between the shots of Bhowali and Igatpuri. The wizards behind this matchless wonder were cinematographer Dilip Gupta and art director Sudhendu Roy. Dilip Gupta has left a vivid account:

'Overall, the outdoors and indoors (which we passed off as outdoors) blended very well in *Madhumati* and it is difficult to detect which is which. You see, we shot the outdoor first and then matched the indoors by maintaining that same quality and source of light, texture and contrast. To be able to do this, we had a number of screenings of the outdoor shots.'

LOVE IN THE MIST

Our visit was nearing its end. The June weather had been anything but pleasant; the rain persisted in holding off while we wilted under the dry heat. Local taxi drivers, waiters and residents wailed in unison; they had not experienced a summer as wicked. But the enchanting pine landscape tempted me to constantly hum the Dilip Kumar remix of the famous Mukesh number: *Suhana safar aur yeh mausam garam*!

Every time Maithili and I walked down the Mall Road, I was enveloped by images from *Madhumati*. Imperious pine trees, the tall mountain ranges, musical bird calls—I was haunted by an uncanny feeling of having walked into a *Madhumati* frame sans the mist casting its diaphanous, romantic spell. But it was not difficult to imagine that ethereal ambience of the hills when mist descends on the valley turning the location into a paradise on earth.

All too quickly, it was our last evening at Ranikhet. Maithili and I had greatly enjoyed our stay. The warm, homely ambience of the old world West View Hotel on Mall Road reminded me of childhood holidays with Baba. I remembered the friendly waiters attending to us and the welcome aroma of freshly cooked food—essential part of a childhood vacation experience. On that last day, my doctor friend Mala[1] inundated me with the contact numbers of several people who had been living in that region since 1950s. I called a few of them, only to discover regretfully that most of them had no idea about *Madhumati* or the fact that a film had been shot in the Kumaon hills fifty-six years ago. My queries drew a blank until I called Raj Shekhar Pant[2].

Destiny was undoubtedly playing a quiet hand. Raj Shekhar Pant was the man I had been looking for! He not only knew of *Madhumati* but also confessed that he had been planning to write a book on the film. *Madhumati* had sentimental memories for the Pant family. Unfortunately, we had no time to meet the kind gentleman who was stationed then in Bhowali as we were leaving early the next morning to catch the train to Delhi. Exchanging contact numbers and email ids was the best option; we promised to continue our association. Secretly I hoped this was not a false start; he seemed to be too good to be true. But luck was on our side, he lived up to his word.

The Pants are a family of professional teachers; I learnt this from his first email. They have a century-old house at Bhimtal named Badri Bhavan, part of a small settlement around 10 kilometres downhill from Bhowali, surrounded by an orchard. Raj Shekhar recollected his father telling him that someone from the *Madhumati* production crew had visited their Bhimtal house with a request to shoot there. The producers were keen to shoot in the Pants' orchard where the peach trees were in full bloom on either side of a gradually ascending garden path and a large circular fish-pond with a statue of Shakuntala adorning the centre. His grandmother, Ganga Devi Pant, vehemently put her feet down; she refused to have film-people shooting in their house. His father, the senior Pant, it seems, had always nursed a secret aspiration to act in films. No permission was granted, and his father's dream of appearing as a minor actor was dashed!

Pant also recalled hearing his father mentioning that local intellectuals were skeptical, in fact critical, of the tribal colour given to hill-life in the film. The semiotics debated included the way the women in the film held their pitchers (earthen pitchers were not common for fetching water in the hills). On the other hand, despite the long stay of the film unit, no misbehaviour was reported. Neither was there any disturbance or even a minor scuffle with locals. Till this day, those old timers who were witness to the shooting cherish wonderful memories of the *Madhumati* cast and crew. They fondly remember Dilip Kumar and the director Bimal Roy who mixed easily with local residents. That they were rather keen on doing so, is what most people from that generation confirmed. Pant adds:

> 'My Father, C.D. Pant, is eighty-eight years old today and my uncle G.C. Pant, eighty-six. Both were teachers at the time in the Leelawati Pant Higher Secondary School when they went to see the shooting of *Madhumati* at Bhowali. The film shooting happened to be a big affair at the time

and no one remembers any other film being shot in the
Kumaon hills before *Madhumati*.'

Pant's father and uncle remember the shooting taking
place along the stretch of the kuccha road connecting Ghorakhal
with the main Bhowali-Bhimtal road. A large part of the
song *Suhana safar* was shot exactly at the spot from where the
trail ascends to the Ghorakhal temple. The summer villa of the
Nawab of Rampur overlooks this temple. (Retaining much of
its original shape, the villa now houses the main office of the
Sainik School Ghorakhal.) Parts of it were shown as the
residences of Pran and Dilip Kumar in the film. The village fair
and the funny scene in which Johnny Walker is hanging upside
down from a tree were also shot in the vicinity. Pant's uncle
remembers a scene in which Dilip Kumar was smoking a bidi.
There were many retakes of the scene as the actor started
coughing badly.

The highlight of Pant's narrative is the curious tale of a local
woman who stood in as Vyjayanthimala's body double. Harish
Chandra Arya had hinted that a local woman was used to run
downhill since the actress was considered too plump! Our
friend Deep vaguely recalled meeting a woman who claimed that
her grandmother had acted in *Madhumati*. But he could not put
a name to her. Raj Shekhar Pant's excellent account of the
incident, naming people and places filled in the blanks. A friend
of the Pants knew a young woman named Yashoda from a
modest background, the daughter of an impoverished man,
one Nari Ram from Gethia. And this according to Pant, is her
story:

> 'A young woman called Yashoda played Vyjayanthimala's
> duplicate in several scenes. One of her scenes involved
> running on a dangerous slope doubling for Vyjayanthimala
> with her back to the camera. This became the talk of the

town. Saroj Sah[3] says Yashoda bore a close resemblance to Vyjayanthimala. She featured in most of the dance sequences. Long after the outdoor shooting of *Madhumati*, Yashoda continued to live in the *Madhumati* character she had enacted. Many locals remember that she could be seen with her curls and locks arranged like *Madhumati*. Yashoda is reported to be dead now. Not much is known about her. The biggest talk of the town in Nainital those days, recalled Saroj Sah, was the massive amount of milk supplied from Nainital to the film unit at Bhowali. Apparently this was required for the bathing of the actress Vyjayanthimala. The elderly people criticized Yashoda and others for working in the film. *Madhumati* was released in Nanital's Ashok Cinema. By the way the film was screened again in the seventies at reduced rates in the very same Ashok Cinema. I was a student at the time and saw the film with my friends, after bunking my class.'

Madhumati is fondly remembered by locals as it was the first Indian film to be shot in the Kumaon region. Consequently, it acquired additional stature. B.R. Chopra shot *Gumrah* (1963) many years later, followed by J.P. Dutta's *Refugee* (2000) which was shot in the Chaubatia area near Ranikhet.

We alighted at the Old Delhi Station on the steamy afternoon of 2 July. Our expedition had been a *Suhana safar* despite minor hiccups. Having experienced a long and tiring journey using three modes of travel, air, train and road—I felt the need to discover why Baba had chosen to take his unit so far away from civilization without an infrastructure or readily available urban comforts.

I had grown up hearing about Mukteshwar from my parents. Later, I read the Jim Corbett stories of man-eaters from these regions. I recalled that Baba's eldest sister—our aunt Jyotsna Sen's family were residents of Muketshwar which is close to

Nainital and only 40 kilometres away from Bhowali. Baba visited his sister frequently, travelling to Kathgodam by train from Lucknow where his other sister, Bibha Sen Roy lived. From Kathgodam, he would trek or go on horseback to Mukteshwar passing through this enchanting magical stretch of uninterrupted pine forests. I am certain that the landscape left indelible imprints on his mind. He was fascinated by the pictorial beauty of the mountains, the forest's majestic charm, its rich musical sounds from those early years in the 1940s. Having seen the splendid photographs he took on these Mukteshwar trips, I am convinced that Baba's decision to choose Bhowali was inspired by his visits to his eldest sister and her husband Shishir Kumar Sen[4] stationed in the region.

Baba, the guru behind *Madhumati*, had simply been bewitched by the beauty of the hills! And on finding a story that matched his dream locale, he transported the entire unit to that distant location.

An old puzzle fell into place once I came to this logical conclusion. The thrill of our *Suhana safar* in Bhowali and Gorakhal will enchant me for a long time. Piecing together the threads of *Madhumati's* film-making history called for a retracing of a journey that I had never personally made with Baba. All the stories woven together here are recollections from a fast-vanishing era. Reading about this long journey I took, in real time and metaphorically, may, just may, enhance *Madhumati's* beguiling charm.

NOTES

[1] My friend, Dr Mala Srikant has moved from New Delhi to Ranikhet and was a true help during the book recce.

[2] Raj Shekhar Pant: see list of contributors.

[3] Sah, Shahs or Sahs have been a leading business community of Kumaon Himalayas. It is believed that they migrated from Nepal.

When Nainital was discovered in the 1840s, they took the responsibility of developing the infrastructural facilities in Nainital. They have been very progressive and are known as the custodians of Kumaoni culture. In regions like Nainital, Bhowali, Dwarahat and Bageshwar, they are still the leading business community.

[4]Shishir Kumar Sen, married to Bimal Roy's eldest sister Jyotsna, headed the Etymology Department of The Imperial Institute of Etymology at Mukteshwar from 1942 to 1948.

7

Film as Dream, Film as Music

No form of art goes beyond ordinary consciousness as cinema does, straight to our emotions, deep into the twilight room of the soul.

—Ingmar Bergman

Our journey into the mythical *Madhumati* land was behind us, and this book on its last leg, when I heard the story how the song *Suhana safar* was created. One day composer Salil Chowdhury and Shailendra drove off to the Khandala Ghats. This hill station was a popular hangout in those days with people of the film industry. As I mentioned earlier, *Madhumati's* opening sequence was shot on one of those hairpin bends at Khandala Ghats. Add to that the new discovery about the creation of *Suhana safar*, thrilled me no end. It was Sonjoy, Salil Chowdhury's son, who told me the interesting anecdote how the opening orchestra bar of *Suhana safar* was conceived:

'Baba and Shailendra had driven up to Khandala one day. As they stood at the top of the Khandala Ghats they saw a goatherd rounding up his flock. The man was making a sharp sound which sounded like *"urrrrrrrrrrrrr"*. On the spot, Baba composed the opening notation for *Suhana safar* including the goatherd's call.'

The fact that *Madhumati's* music throbs in my veins, makes it difficult for me to talk dispassionately. I was, at first, diffident to comment on the musical legacy of *Madhumati's* music. Yet its outstanding music cannot be excluded in a book exploring specifics about the film. In fact, its music can be the subject of an entire volume, if not a single chapter.

Not being knowledgeable about music, I drew on the experience of individuals eminently suited to talk on the subject and share their insights about *Madhumati's* music. The film's music, I think, can be easily discussed in two segments—the songs as separate from the background score. Composer Tushar Bhatia, an ardent admirer of Salil Chowdhury and Bimal Roy, summed it up succinctly saying 'the background score of *Madhumati* is like a Bible for us music composers'.

Repeated viewing of the film made me wonder why the phenomenal background score had not been included as part of the film's music collection? The discs of Hollywood musicals include the background score in the audio CDs. Could our record companies not follow the example?

Madhumati's outstanding orchestration, its musical movements from andante to allegro—the intensely poignant passages could have been scored by Wolfgang Amadeus Mozart. The mention of Mozart brings to surface the stories I heard from music critic Kishore Chatterjee[1] or Kishoreda, as we called him. Kishoreda was openly dismissive of mainstream Bombay cinema, in fact, he mischievously dubbed it oriental opera! He watched a Hindi film only if its music attracted him. After watching *Madhumati* in Dehradun, Kishoreda fell head over heels in love with its songs. The folksy composition *Chadh gayo paapi bichua* bowled him over so completely that he decided to watch the film a second time—an honour that he seems to have bestowed only upon *Madhumati*. Madly obsessed with this song, he haunted the music shops of Kolkata in order to buy the long playing record (LP) of *Madhumati*. Kishoreda recalls:

'When I told my friends *Bichua* was intensely Mozartian, they brushed me off. I am fairly certain now that Salil did indeed, cleverly and creatively, mingle folk melodies with the Mozartian sense of perpetual movement, which can be termed a divine momentum. Salil must have studied Mozart allegros carefully before composing this song. In *Bichua*, I find the contest and interaction or struggle between the soloist and the chorus that recurs in a Mozart concerto...the connection between Mozart and Salil's tune fascinated me. Only a classical symphony has this lilt, it is found in Mozart, Haydn and Schmitz. Salil Chowdhury romanticized Mozart. I am not a regular filmgoer. Yet the music of *Madhumati* literally dragged me to the film.'

Elaborating on the influence of western classical composers on Salil Chowdhury's style is pertinent. It offers an insight into his immense grasp over his art, his vast knowledge of the western maestros. In some of Salil Chowdhury's compositions, east and west meet in perfect harmony, a musical marriage. The lilting *Chhaya* (1961) duet, for example, *Itna na mujhse tu pyar badha* is a much discussed composition adapted from Mozart's Symphony No. 40 in G Minor.

Bichua, that lively duet sung by Manna Dey and Lata Mangeshkar, is a sheer delight and one of the film's highlights. Manna Dey, known for his mirth and wry humour, shared[2] an interesting story about his gifted fellow-singer, Lata Mangeshkar:

'We were singing a duet for Salil Chowdhury—a very entertaining song *Aiso re paapi bichua* for Bimalda's *Madhumati*. Lata was asked to give some sort of an expression at one point in the song. I sang a line and as I finished, she sang: Oye-oye-oye-oyee...or something like that. I was taken aback and stopped. Lata is alive to all situations, and as far as her singing is concerned, ask her to express any situation, she can do it. I think she does justice to every song.'

Suhana Safar, the signature tune of *Madhumati* was sung by the golden-voiced Mukesh. It is believed that the singer originally intended for this iconic song was Talat Mehmood. Mukeshji, it seems, was going through a financial crunch. His situation prompted Talat Mehmood to suggest that the song be given to Mukesh. I have heard this story twice to be convinced about its authenticity—first from Mrs Talat Mehmood, later an independent confirmation by Sanjoy Chowdhury. Nitin Mukesh once announced that his father's comeback song was *Yeh mera diwanapan hai* from a lesser known Bimal Roy film, *Yahudi*, starring Dilip Kumar. The 1950s period in the Indian film industry was marked by a generosity of spirit and well-being among fellow artists. The cut-throat competition of today was relatively unknown.

Maithili Rao puts her finger unerringly on the right spot when she says that the haunting music of *Madhumati* is almost as a parallel narrative track. It is as if the narrative moves in a perpetual waltz from present into the past through flashbacks and reminiscences. A pulsating background score matches the tenor of visual language. From start to finish, a continuous jugalbandi between the layered musical score and the narrative thread flows into the story. As the film progresses through many twists and turns towards the astonishing finale, the music and image compliment one other. In no other film of my father have I found this delicate balance between the music and image, except *Madhumati*. Renowned film-maker Ingmar Bergman believed that a film had the potential to match the abstract state of music. *Madhumati* achieves that state of abstraction by passages of pictorial lyricism.

Madhumati's songs continue to enchant generations of listeners. Before I continue on the musical trail let me regale readers with another interesting story. It was strongly hinted that Salil Chowdhury was not amongst the original contenders considered to compose the music of *Madhumati* despite the fact that the composer's brilliance was established beyond doubt with *Do Bigha Zamin* (his debut film). It is pertinent to mention here that he had also authored the story of *Do Bigha Zamin*. However, the vagaries of the film industry caused Salil Chowdhury to be declared a flop music director by Bombay's populist standards.

Bimal Roy worked alternately with two composers and the two were Sachin Dev Burman and Salil Chowdhury. When *Madhumati* was still in the pipeline, S.D. Burman had already been assigned to compose music for *Sujata* which followed *Madhumati*. It was Salil Chowdhury's turn therefore, to compose for *Madhumati*; he had been closely involved with the project, attending script sessions and going on locations. But in the final stage of the project, film distributors who advance funds, fiercely opposed Salil Chowdhury. Distributors had a big stake in films and their word was invariably law. They argued that in a project ostensibly designed for the box office there was no room for a flop music director. It was rumoured that Dilip Kumar, *Madhumati*'s hero, was vehemently opposed to Salil Chowdhury as a composer.

Gossip spreads like wildfire within the industry and when Dilip's Kumar's opposition became known, Salil Chowdhury and Shailendra were taken aback. Dilip Kumar's resistance raised serious doubts about their talent, but the two refused to buckle and braced themselves to create magical music. Their determination was boosted by Baba's infinite faith in them. And Baba confirmed his faith in Salil Chowdhury in his quiet manner, by signing Salil Chowdhury! The rest, as they say, is history.

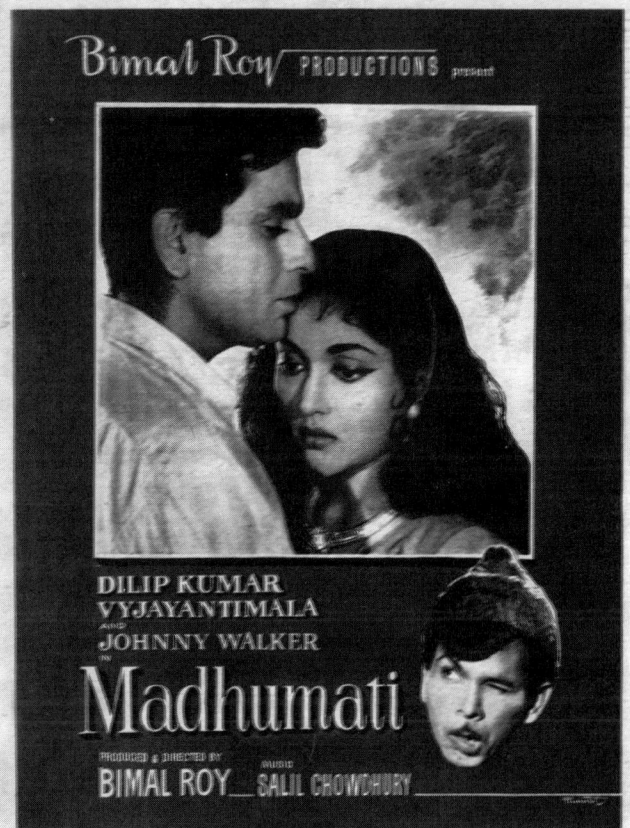

Madhumati's pre-release publicity poster
Courtesy: Author archives

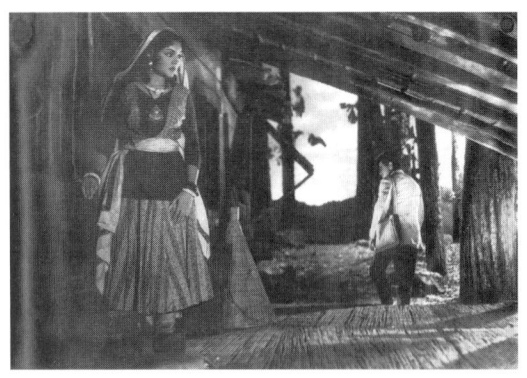

Anand leaving Madhumati's (Vyjayanthimala)
home at night
Courtesy: Kamat Foto Flash

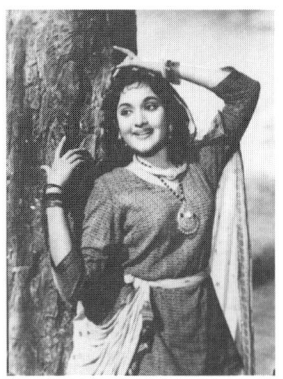

The beautiful Vyjayanthimala as Madhumati
Courtesy: Kamat Foto Flash

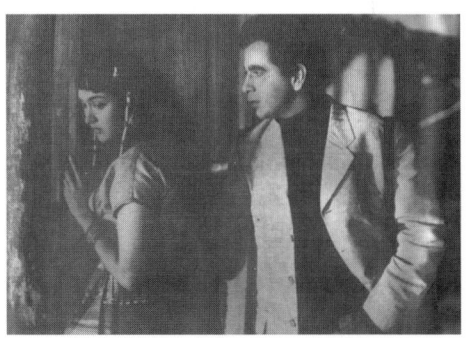

Anand and Madhumati
at her home
Courtesy: Kamat Foto
Flash

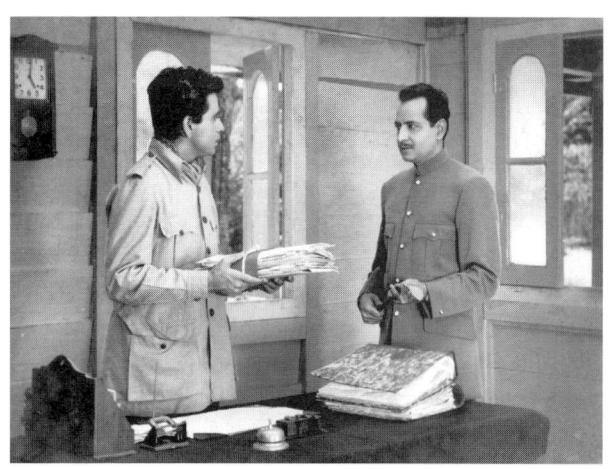

Ugranarayan (Pran) confronts Anand (Dilip Kumar)
Courtesy: Kamat Foto Flash

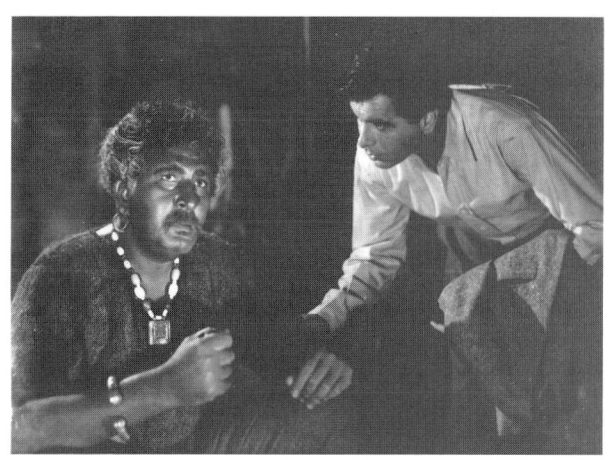

Jayant, as Madhumati's father, with Dilip Kumar as Anand
Courtesy: Kamat Foto Flash

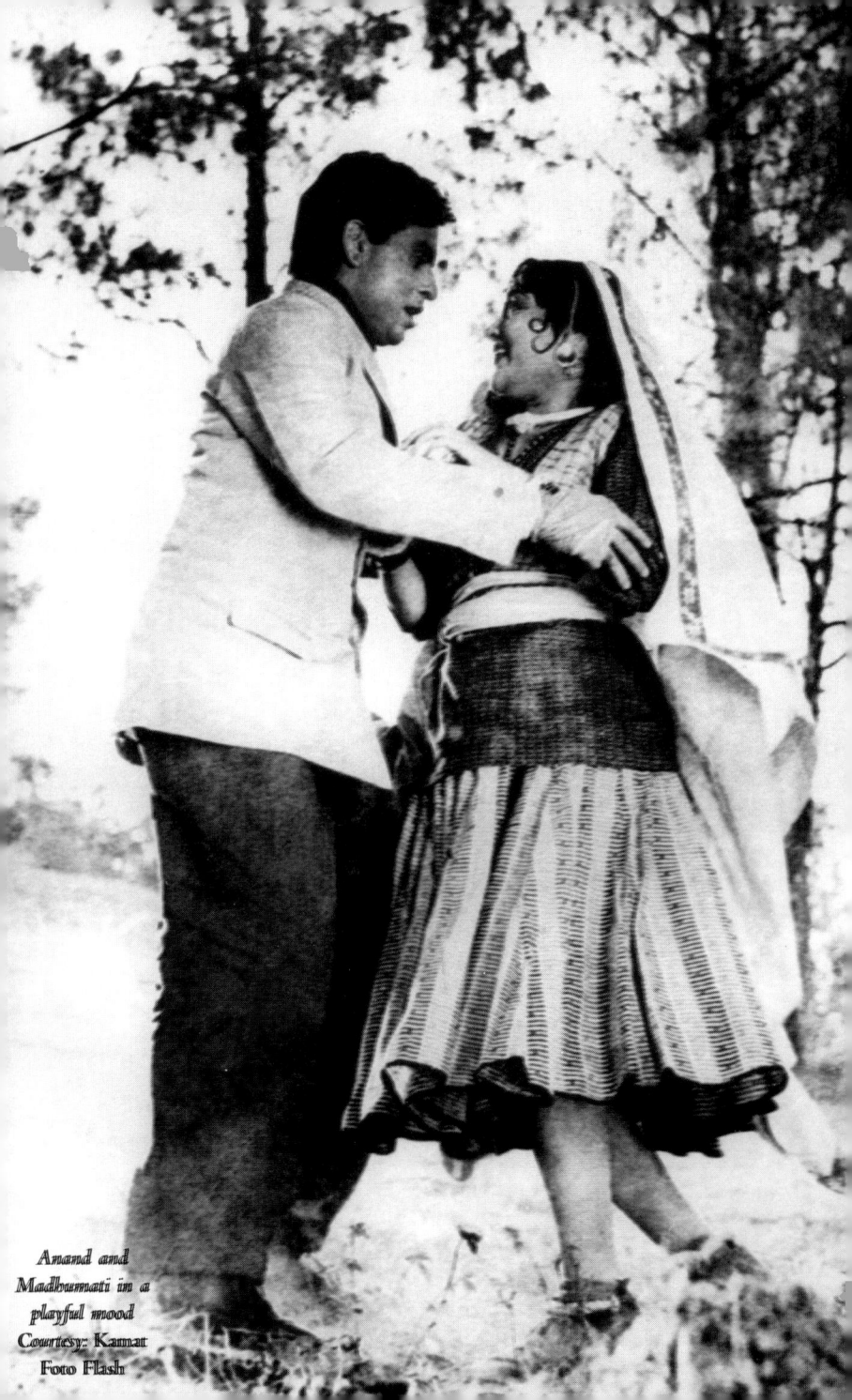

Anand and Madhumati in a playful mood
Courtesy: Kamat Foto Flash

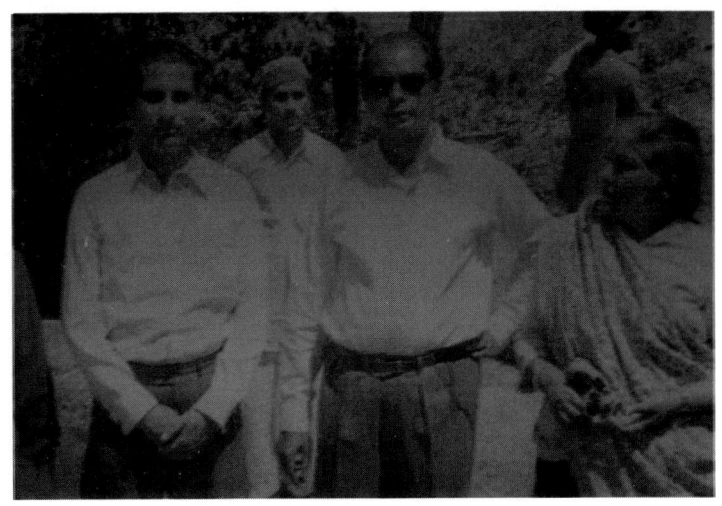

Bimal Roy with some local people of Ghorakhal
Courtesy: Raj S. Pant

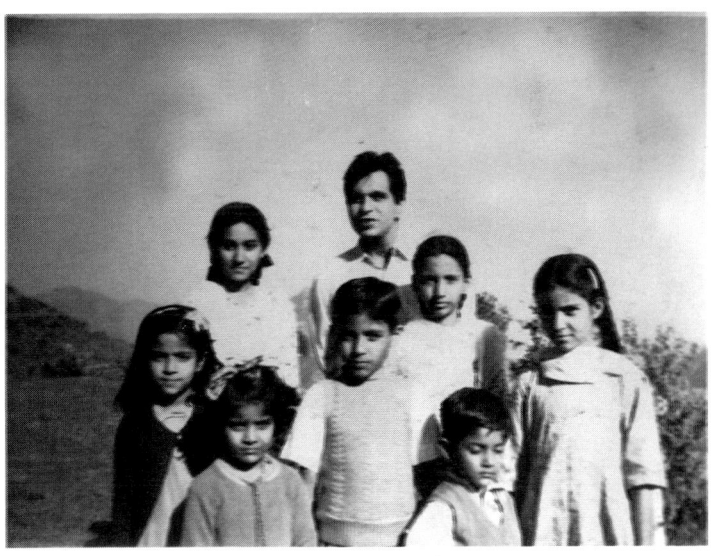

Dilip Kumar at Madhumati's outdoor location shoot with
Dr Razia Husain on his left, and her siblings
Courtesy: Author archives

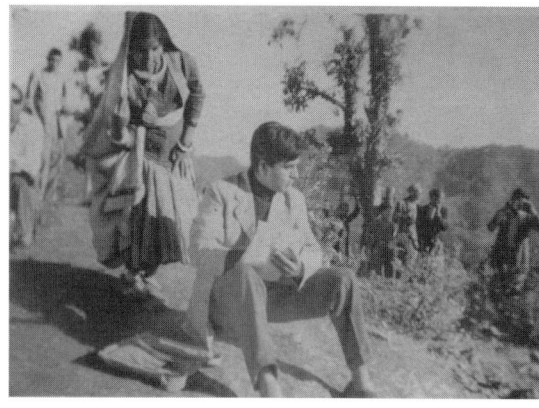

Dilip Kumar's photograph taken during an outdoor shoot of Madhumati *Courtesy:* Dr Razia Husain

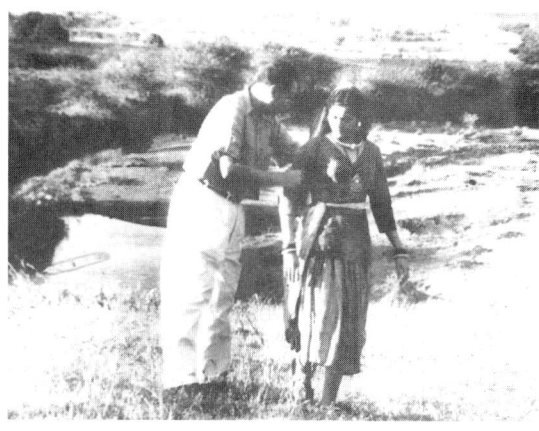

Bimal Roy directing Vyjayanthimala on location Courtesy: Author archives

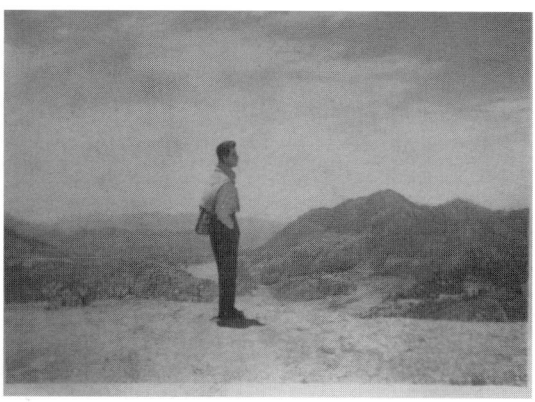

At the Ghorakhal location Courtesy: Dr Razia Husain

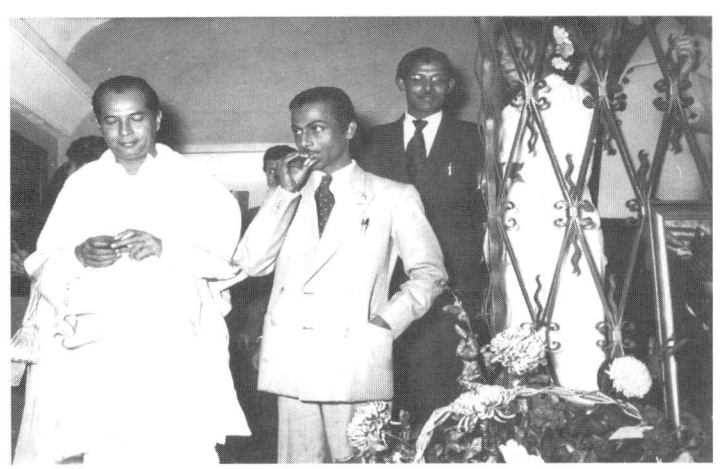

(L to R) Bimal Roy, Salil Chowdhury and Hrishikesh Mukherjee
Courtesy: Author archives

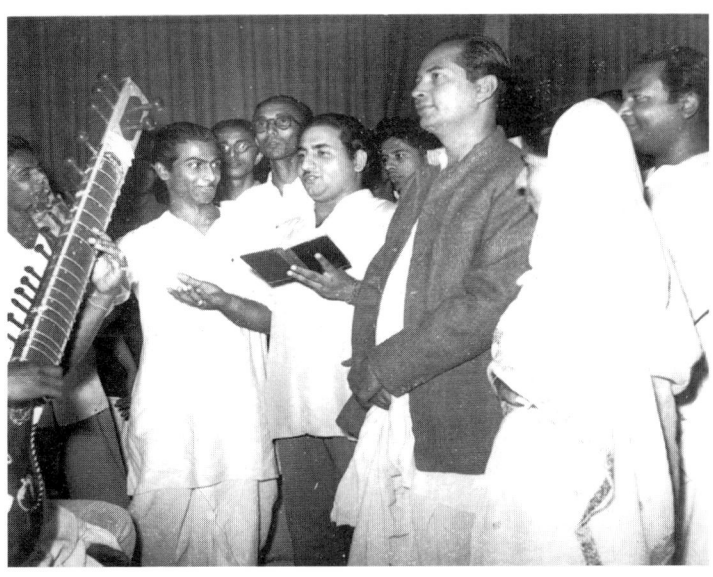

(L to R) Front: Kanu Ghosh, Salil Chowdhury, Mohd. Rafi, Bimal Roy, Asit
Sen (at the back) and Lata Mangeshkar
Courtesy: Author archives

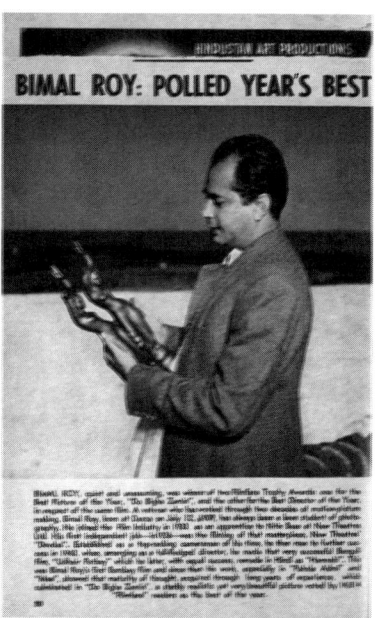

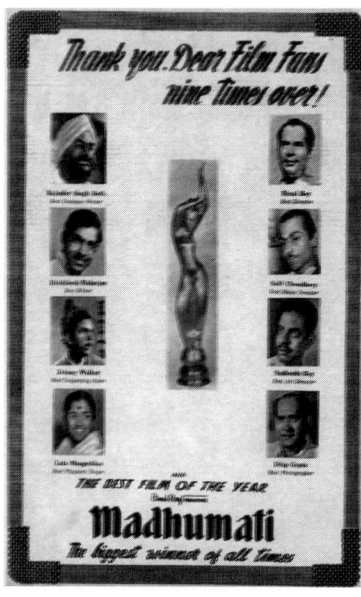

*Promotional material for Madhumati,
announcing its nine Filmfare awards
Courtesy: Author archives*

*Bimal Roy with his first two Filmfare
Awards for Do Bigha Zamin (Best Film
and Best Director, 1954)
Courtesy: Author archives*

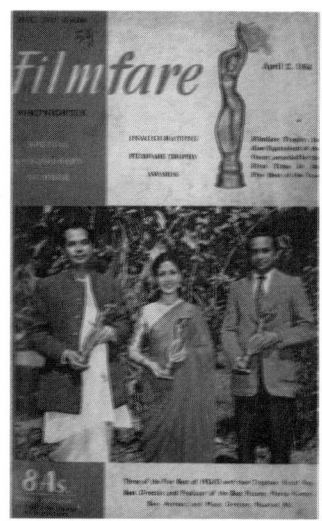

*The Filmfare cover after the first
Filmfare Awards
Courtesy: Author archives*

After the release of *Madhumati*, the composer Salil Chowdhury signed no less than nineteen films.

Another anecdote, replete with the grace of that bygone era comes to mind. Salil Chowdhury enjoyed a warm relationship with veteran S.D. Burman. After *Madhumati* was released, he carried its 33 rpm long playing record as a gift to the senior composer. The record played on the three in one system as S.D. closed his eyes in rapt attention. When the music came to an end, S.D. came back to earth and shifted the paan in his mouth from one cheek to the other before turning to Sholil, as he called Salil Chowdhury to deliver his verdict: 'Sholil, if they still call you a flop, just pack up and go back to Kolkata!'

Not only were the two composers cordial to one another, they were often present during each other's music recordings. Composer Pyarelal, a music hand those days, remembers their discussion about including the chirping of birds in the opening bar of *Suhana Safar*. It was at S.D.'s suggestion, says Pyarelal, that the chirping of birds preceded the music of the song.

Music Composer Shantanu Moitra[3] is full of admiration for that early era:

> 'It was Bimal Roy who introduced me to Salil Chowdhury through his films and till today I remain one of Salilda's biggest fans. In *Suhana safar*, the arrangement and the sound design go hand in hand, the chirping of the birds, the use of the flute and the unmistakable "Ohoho" which sounds like an echo in the valley that is immediately followed by the beautiful line, *Woh aasman jhuk raha hai zameen par…*, a simple sound technique to highlight the idea of paradise on earth. This was possible because the director, the lyricist and the music composer sat and worked on the songs together. Bimalda loved, understood and enjoyed creating and picturizing songs.'

These observations by a modern composer are relevant if we are to understand the fine ethical concerns that artists shared indeed accorded one another. It is well-known that amongst Lata's repertory, the song *Aaja re main toh kab se khadi is paar*, holds an unique position. A special mention of the song and the response it evoked is recorded in the book written on Lata Mangeshkar by Nasreen Munni Kabir. I quote that entire portion:

'I am still very fond of *Madhumati*.

NMK: I always felt there is a certain similarity between *Mahal* and *Madhumati*. Though their stories develop quite differently, both films start in similar settings. A terrible storm is raging and the hero in *Mahal* and *Madhumati* take shelter in an old dilapidated house and discover a painting that stirs up a distant past, another lifetime. *Aayega aanewala* and *Aaja re pardesi* are also used in both films to create the same effect—evoking a romantic past and spiritual bond between hero and heroine. Was *Aaja re pardesi* a difficult song to get right?

LM: Actually it was recorded very quickly. I don't think it took more than a few hours. Shailendraji was very happy with the way I sang it, so he gave me a huge bunch of flowers! And Bimalda held my hand in appreciation. I was fond of Salilda's compositions because they were very difficult. Whether based on folk music or his imagination, his songs had so many high and low notes that sometimes the musicians would get flustered. But I enjoyed singing for him.

NMK: Bimal Roy's songs are also beautifully embedded in story-telling. Did you have many discussions with him?

LM: I didn't discuss songs directly with Bimalda. He talked in Bengali and I hardly spoke it at the time. He was a serious and quiet man and never talked much. He sat quietly at the recording studio and all he would say to me in Bengali was: "*Namashkar.* How are you? Well?" Nothing more than that!

I liked his films. Whether his songs were good or bad wasn't important—the whole film was good. I consider him among our great directors.'

Prasoon Joshi[4], a sensitive and popular lyricist of the current age, believes Bimal Roy had the ability to choreograph music into the narrative, saying:

'Bimal Roy had the ability to speak through his songs. The songs meant so much for each of the films. *Aaja re* in *Madhumati* came at a critical juncture. It was the revelation, the first introduction of Madhumati's intriguing character. This could have been done through dialogues or a third-person narration or a voice-over of a third person, but Bimal Roy uses a song. It intertwines so beautifully with the situation that one cannot think of the situation without the song.'

On the occasion of Baba's ninety-eighth birth anniversary, we invited the multi-faceted Shekhar Sen[5] to speak about the music of Bimal Roy's films. He enthralled the audience by his persuasive, scholarly analysis. His lecture demonstration highlighting the importance of the 1950s and 60s in the history of Indian cinema. Sen considers that particular period an extremely important time for art lovers, urging us to learn from that era:

'In the Shastras it is said: "To send an arrow far, place it on the bow and pull it right back; the more you pull it back, the further it will go." Similarly, the more we learn from our past and our history, I feel, our future will turn more beautiful as our past is beautiful.

The songs of *Madhumati* were super hits and there are long discussions on their merits among music-lovers. One song which was less popular but according to me—and I salute Salilda for composing it—is simply unique. This song is placed in a strange situation. I doubt if it is possible for another film-maker to even imagine such a situation. That song is: *Daiya re daiya chadh gayo paapi bichua*.

I request you to watch this song carefully. You will observe when Mannada begins to sing his piece, a tantric enters the scene. He is also a ghost-buster. Bimalda and Mannada have captured the situation beautifully. The viewers receive the impression that this man playing the tantric is not an actor but a real tantric and chasing ghosts has always been his sole occupation. In the song Mannada has marvelously used his expressive voice. Listen to the song and feel it. This is not merely a song; no it is not merely a song, I repeat. The song does not rise from the singer's throat—it emerges directly from his heart to reach out and captivate the listeners.'

Shekhar Sen had the last word on the film-makers of that era when he commented that it would be a mistake to call Bimal Roy just a film-maker: 'In that epoch, they were complete artistes; they were not just film-makers. If I say for Bimalda that he was only a film-maker, I will be doing him a great injustice. He was a complete artiste.'

Madhumati is an indisputed part of the mythology of Indian cinema. It has to be considered a celluloid icon by virtue of its qualification as a complete work of artistic unity.

NOTES

[1]Kishore Chatterjee, *The Statesman* art/music critic wrote in his chapter 'Mozart and Madhumati' in *Bimal Roy: The Man Who Spoke in Pictures*, ed. Rinki Roy Bhattacharya.

[2]*Lata Mangeshkar…In her own voice*, by Nasreen Munni Kabir (Niyogi Books, 2009).

[3]For further reading, Shantanu Moitra's essay: 'Bimal Roy and

Hindi Film Music', pg 84/85, in *Bimal Roy: The Man Who Spoke in Pictures*, ed. Rinki Roy Bhattacharya.

[4]For further reading, Prasoon Joshi's essay: 'Music and Lyrics in the Films of Bimal Roy', pg 80/81, in *Bimal Roy: The Man Who Spoke in Pictures*, ed. Rinki Roy Bhattacharya.

[5]Shekhar Sen, a talented singer, music composer, lyricist and actor, was brought up in a Bengali family of Raipur, Chhattisgarh. He was fortunate to learn music from his parents, late Dr Arun Kumar Sen and late Dr Aneeta Sen renowned classical singers of the Gwalior Gharana and musicologists. Shekhar established himself as a singer with a different style by singing the medieval poets like Raskhan, Raheem, Lalitkishori, Bhooshan Bihari and many more. To his credit, he has performed in more than twelve hundred singing concerts all over the world, released more than two hundred cassettes and CDs as singer, composer and lyricist. He composed music in many TV serials like *Shiv Mahapuran, Geeta Rahasya, Parivaar, Dhadkan* etc. and given playback in the famous serial *Ramayan*. He then invented a new style in the field of entertainment. His mono-act musical plays *Tulsi, Kabeer, Vivekanand* and *Saahab* created history with more than six hundred shows in India, USA, UK, Belgium, Hongkong, Singapore, Indonesia, Trinidad & Suriname. The quest never ends, therefore as a true representative of Indian culture Shekhar moves ahead in search of new horizons.

8

Looking Back

In retrospect, our trip to Bhowali and Ranikhet was a step in the right direction. It revealed a great deal about the actual *Madhumati* location besides other trivia. For several years I had carried the impression that the film had been shot in Nainital. Our visit demolished that myth effectively.

At the end of the journey, there still remained one grey area—the film's budget. Professional fees of Bollywood stars always arouse wild speculations; that was an even bigger riddle. I often wondered how much the leading stars were paid. Assistant editor, the chatterbox Sakharam Borsay, casually quipped one day: 'Guess how much Vyjayanthimala was paid for *Madhumati*, Rinki didi! Did you know she was paid more than Dilip Kumar? Vyjayanthimala was paid almost fifty thousand!'

Once a film attains the stature of a legend, or earns the distinction of a celluloid classic, myths are invented around it. Most of these stories turn out to be baseless in the end. I paid no attention to Sakharam's story, though his remark made me curious. It seemed inappropriate on my part to address any questions to Vyjayanthimala in this regard. But the thought persisted—had she actually received more than her mega star hero?

Many believed that Bimal Roy had no choice but to make a commercially designed film like *Madhumati* with the precise objective of saving Bimal Roy Productions. It was also believed that unless he succumbed to commercial demands, Bimal Roy Productions would suffer heavy collateral damage; perhaps collapse for good. My husband, director Basu Bhattacharya, was fairly certain this was the case. In a Channel 4 TV interview, my mother Monobina Roy went on to say that it was the ghost story, *Madhumati*, which raked in resources. Such stories voiced by important individuals, my mother for example, were in the air when I began to take serious interest about the complex business of making films and the even more complex business of financial implications.

But the crucial question, *Madhumati's* budget, remained an elusive mystery like *Madhumati* herself! Was there a budget at all for the film? How was the original budget structured? And what was the additional amount required to complete the film? Importantly, how did the project generate funds? These grey areas had no answers in sight when I began writing the book.

My curiosity about this particular aspect made me track down the elusive Mr Amrit Shah, almost ninety-years-old and the erstwhile BRP manager. He was a key individual, having handled the finances, but my efforts to track him down proved fruitless. Watching my brother's documentary[1] on Baba, Mr Shah's sound bites affirmed an unworldly Bimalda, completely hopeless at business! I decided to ask my younger sister Aparajita, to find out all she could from Mr Shah about the economics of the film. He had, after all, handled BRP's administrative department.

My sister managed to glean the information that *Devdas*, BRP's previous production, had been made at a budget of about twelve lakhs. This sum excluded making the final prints. *Madhumati's* original budget was fifteen lakhs but the film ended up costing close to twenty five lakhs. Amrit Shah went on record to say that much of this additional expense was due to unforeseen problems at the *Madhumati* location shooting in the hills. A large chunk of the outdoor footage shot in Bhowali had to be junked. New locations had to be recreated in Mohan Studios. The studio re-shoot posed other predictable problems like a long wait for fresh dates from its busy stars. Due to all this, the film's budget went completely haywire.

Mr Shah's personal opinion was that *Madhumati* was made with funds from BRP; the overflow from the *Devdas* production was perhaps initially channelized to fund *Madhumati*. In Mr Shah's words, BRP was 'not a fat, rich production house'. At the same time, he hesitated to call it poor. These sketchy details left me dissatisfied; however, I had no other source who could have given me authentic details.

Looking back, I realize how exceptionally fortunate I was in gathering rare nuggets for this book. Discovering the three eyewitnesses, Dr Razia Husain, Professor Raj Shekhar Pant and the cleaner Mangulal, made a significant difference. Their memories were invaluable in fleshing and colouring the making of *Madhumati* in the Kumaon region.

Last month I struck gold once more, chatting with writer Sanjit Narwekar[2]. Aware that I was writing about *Madhumati*, he drew my attention to Bunny Reuben's[3] book[4] on Dilip Kumar. Reuben had included the first-hand account of a gentleman named Premji[5] about the *Madhumati* outdoor shooting in his book. I remember Premji, of course.

During his research for the Dilip Kumar book, Reuben had spoken to several individuals from the film industry including a gentleman who was simply known as Premji. If I recall rightly, Premji always dressed in white and had been Dilip Kumar's secretary for a while. I remember him too, from the group photographs taken on recce trips to Nainital to find outdoor locations for *Madhumati*. It suddenly dawned on me that Premji was part of the *Madhumati* production team. I searched frantically through the credits of *Madhumati* and drew a blank.

Premji's account, with its fine details, is a rare, authentic report about the *Madhumati* shooting, documented in Bunny Reuben's book. He has talked about vital aspects, the post-production problems that Baba faced, including the financial debacle which almost stalled *Madhumati*. His account opens up an entirely unknown aspect of *Madhumati* besides emphasizing the tremendous respect Baba commanded in the Indian film industry. Premji's account follows:

'During the 45-day long outdoor schedule for Bimal Roy's *Madhumati* in Nainital, I came in close contact with Dilip Kumar who was cast opposite Vyjayanthimala. The entire unit of the film was stationed at Nainital and as the man in charge of production, I had to cater to everyone's needs. There were hundreds of members but our entire unit lived like one family. Nainital was not as developed then as it is today. From a pin to petrol, I had to run down the hill to the shopping centre to get things. Large quantities of smoke bombs were needed to create fog in the filming of the songs. With great difficulty I would manage to get the smoke bombs from the local Defence Department. Dilip Kumar respected Bimal Roy greatly. He was co-operative on the sets, made sure there was no problem from his side. Bimal Roy was a perfectionist and would shoot in the most difficult of places to get an authentic atmosphere and explore nature's beauty. Dilip and Vyjayanthimala, on whom four songs were filmed, were enthusiastic in doing the scenes in all sorts of odd places. Bimal Roy was worried, due to the 45-day long schedule, the film had gone over budget by about eight to ten lakhs. And Bimalda was not the kind of person who would raise his price. He had permanent distributors he trusted. How then to meet the deficit? Dilip Kumar came to know this. He did not want a film-maker of Bimalda's calibre to be burdened with financial problems. He knew Bimal Roy was a good film-maker, but a bad businessman. He told Bimalda not to worry but arrange for a preview for all his distributors, followed by a luncheon. After the show and lunch, Dilip rose to speak. He told the distributors why the film had gone over-budget and why Bimal Roy was worried. He announced that he would forego Rs 70,000 that was due to him from Bimal Roy to ease the burden. He asked the distributors whether they would like to contribute. Chotubhai Desai, a reputed Delhi distributor, was the first one to come forward saying he would match whatever Dilip Kumar had forgone. The other distributors came forward and the deficit of ten lakh rupees was met. As expected, the film was a big hit and the distributors were very happy.'

Premji's account speaks of exemplary men in halcyon times. A moral tale which reminds us that faith moves mountains. Had Dilip Kumar not played the Good Samaritan or conducted the lunch diplomacy during that bleak period, *Madhumati* may have remained in cans. His high regard for Baba prompted the star to take a leading part in averting a fatal blow to the film.

Madhumati belongs to Hindi cinema's *Belle Époque*. This is a tribute to the profound faith that all concerned had for that unique creation called *Madhumati*.

With these words, I formally conclude my tribute to the magnificent film and its makers.

NOTES

[1] A documentary film by Sonjoy Roy, titled *Remembering Bimal Roy*.
[2] Sanjit Narwekar is a National Award-winning film historian, author, publisher and documentary film-maker with more than four decades of cross-media experience in journalism, public relations, publishing and film-making. He has a passion for film history and has

written/edited thirty-plus books including *Marathi Cinema: In Retrospect* (1995), which received the Swarna Kamal in 1996 as the Best Cinema Book of the Year.

[3]See list of contributors.

[4]For further reading: *Dilip Kumar, Star Legend of Indian Cinema*, the definitive biography by Bunny Reuben (Harper Collins).

[5]Producer, Production Manager Premji: Produced nine films including *Mera Saaya* (1966), *Dushman* (1971), *Imaan Dharam* (1977), *Majboor* (1974).

II

Other Voices

A Tribute

Among many other creative regrets that I have, is the missed opportunity of not having had the honour of working with one of India's finest directors, Mr Bimal Roy. Bimalda, as he was affectionately called, passed away long before my time. But his rich legacy remained with me.

The body of work he left behind for us, indeed, for the entire industry, adequately reflects his complete control over the medium. It also gives us a fairly accurate insight into his unique personality. I have come to believe that an individual's character is reflected in the way in which he or she embraces creativity. Though I did not have the opportunity to meet Bimalda, I was able to formulate an idea of what he was like as a private individual—thanks to the kindness of Mr Hrishikesh Mukherjee. Hrishida, one of his most illustrious assistants, worked as the editor of most Bimal Roy films till he took over direction himself. During the course of the several films that Hrishida and I worked together, frequent renditions of Bimalda's genius would feature in our conversation. The subtlety of story-telling for example, or a particular editing cut that he suggested, a certain lighting style or altered camera angle he would consider before taking a shot documents his eye for detail. All this was told with immense respect from the point of view of his *shishya*—Hrishida.

From the vast repertoire of Bimalda's films, two stand out luminously in my mind as exceptional—*Devdas* and *Sujata*. No doubt, his entire work fell under an 'exceptional category', but these two films have remained with me forever.

Devdas is a renowned literary work, celebrated cinematically by its previous celluloid versions. But for me, Bimal Roy's *Devdas* was a film that stirred in a novice what cinema ought to be. At that early stage in life I admit, I had no idea, no intention of joining the profession. However, even at that impressionable young age, the film created an image that resembled reality in an otherwise unreal medium. I have to admit, although, that much of my first impression of *Devdas* was due to the presence of Dilip Kumar. The actor is an inspiration, idolized by me for his flawless performances. Later, I became aware of many other finer aspects of film; I discovered the nuances of time, cause and reason behind what went on to make the performances appreciated. The credit for this belonged to the one who wielded the baton, the director. Not just the performance, many aspects of the story-telling were immediately identifiable.

It was apparent that even in situations of grim tragedy, thanks to the nature of its representation, one would smile at its actuality, when it would have been appropriate perhaps to be taken in by the sadness of the moment.

There is one particular scene I wish to offer as an example— when Devdas (Dilip Kumar) is shown wrapped in mourning after his father's death. A griefstricken Devdas is sitting alone— into that solemn frame enters a wailing mourner walking up to him, shedding crocodile tears. The nuanced manner in which Dilip Kumar's imperceptible hand movement directs the mourner to another part of the home, to his brother was brilliant cinematic execution. It was not just the performance but the very concept of the scene that deserves applause. My appreciation of Motilal as an exceptional actor has been credited to Bimal Roy. Notably, the finest moments of a performance are often the contribution of the director.

In his stories, Bimalda addressed complex social problems that confront our society. Indian society is reeling under these very issues despite sixty-six years of independence. *Sujata* is one such film, providing an insight to the existing caste issue. The film's major asset was a portrayal of stellar strength by Nutan, who is also one of my favourite actors.

To keep faith in one's own stamp of creation within the excesses of the commercial escapist mainstream cinema is an inordinately difficult task. But Bimalda did not compromise or relent. I would like to believe what came to be addressed as 'the middle path' cinema, years later, had its roots in the thinking and films of Bimal Roy.

Hrishida always spoke of Bimalda as a gentle, considerate and softhearted man. Had he not educated me on this aspect of Bimalda's nature, I would have discovered it myself in the films made by him. There was a soft fluidity in his frames and a gentle mobility in the camera movements. Harshness found no residence in his nature of work.

Bimalda's brilliance was recognized often by awards. It is no wonder then that among the entire history of directors in the Indian film industry, at least in Hindi cinema, he was awarded always as the best, the maximum number of times.

Amitabh Bachchan

An Unexpected Night[1]

Aapke saath guzara hua lamha,
Lutf lene baithoon, toh zindagi kam hai…

This is a story that belongs to an era when battery-operated radios were slowly being eased out to be replaced by electronic radios. The year was 1963.

It was a cold December day when I was sitting outside Shankar Tripathi's radio shop, Shankar Radios, enjoying the winter sunshine. Sitting there, at peace with the world, I was attempting to sketch the diagram of an electronic condenser when the errant power-supply returned and the radio sprang to life with an old song from the film *Madhumati*: *Suhaana safar aur yeh mausam haseen!*

Shailendra's lyrics composed melodiously by Salil Chowdhury and rendered in Mukesh's silky voice warmed the mellow winter sunshine. Till today, the memory of that delicate moment remains dew-fresh in my heart and mind.

Trying to pluck the delicate petals of moments from a distant past and frame, those tender images of a bygone era into words has proved formidable. But I intend to give it my best try…

Mukesh was singing the last lines of the song when Shankar Tripathiji asked me: 'Gyan, do you know which film that song was from?'

'Yes,' I replied, 'it is from *Madhumati*.'

I have been fond of films from my childhood. After a pause I added: 'Bhaisahab, I can also tell you the name of the lyricist, the singer and the music-director.'

He smiled gently: 'But Gyan, I know a special thing or two about this film which few know.'

'What is that special thing?' I asked Shankarji.

My question brought a warm glow in his eyes. He stood up and said simply, 'Come let us move inside and continue chatting.'

As we stepped inside, Shankarji turned off the radio and I pulled up a chair to sit beside him, asking: 'Bhaisahab, is it about Bimal Roy, the director of *Madhumati*?'

'Yes, Gyan,' he replied, 'I will tell you something about the same Bimal Roy. The chair on which you are sitting is the very chair on which Bimalda sat one night from 10 pm to 4 am the next morning.'

Congratulating my good fortune, I settled more comfortably on the chair before querying, 'But, Bhaisahab, which of Bimal Roy's radios was not working that he had to sit on this seat with you all night?'

Scarcely had I posed the question when Tripathiji's wife entered the room and placed our lunch on the table. My attention was diverted as I said, 'Let us continue the anecdote after we finish lunch.'

Had Tripathiji not related the anecdote that winter noon, I would not have entered it into the filmy diary I carry inside my head…but he had continued:

'Gyan, as you know, my daily routine is to leave for home the minute I close the shop and that day was no different. I had barely shut the shop when a car drew up and a man stepped out and asked me something.'

'Sir, are you the owner of Shankar Radios?' (Perhaps he had seen me locking up the shop). 'We have heard,' he continued, 'that you have also been a wireless radio operator.'

I replied in a curt, dry manner: 'What business is it of yours?'

A second man stepped out of the car now and approaching me, said: 'Excuse me, but please do not be so curt with us. We have come all the way from Bombay to make a film in your town. An important part of our sound-recorder is not working. We need your help urgently.'

'I am going home right now,' I said in a busy voice. 'I will see what I can do tomorrow morning.'

I was about to turn away, when the first man spoke again: 'It will be too late for us, Sir. Please agree to do the repair tonight. You will be given more money than you ask for.'

'I work purely for satisfaction and peace of mind. Temptation of money, I am afraid, will disturb my peace of mind.'

When he heard me say this, the second man, dressed in a long overcoat, pulled at his cigarette deeply before speaking with great simplicity: 'Forgive me, but satisfaction and peace of mind are the shadows of money, is it not so?'

These strange words made me look at him with greater interest. His words had a powerful ring to them.

He stubbed out his cigarette against an electricity pole before turning to me: 'Have you heard of Bimal Roy?'

I shook my head to signify I had not. The first man spoke now: 'What about names like Dilip Kumar and Vyjayanthimala? You have surely heard of them?'

'Yes,' I replied, 'I have seen many of their films.'

'Bimalda is currently making a film with them here.'

Upon hearing this, I opened my shop while two other men got down from the car to stand beside Bimalda, who said: 'These two men will help you with the work.'

I switched on the light and Bimalda sat on that chair while his companions sat on benches resting against the wall and other chairs. Two assistants brought in the faulty machine and placed it on the table. Drawing the table lamp closer, I switched it on and began to examine each part, oblivious to all of them now.

One of the assistants drew out a huge book from a bag to read it carefully and was about to give me some information when I stopped him: 'Please close that. I do not need a book.'

He shut the book and laid it aside.

I took out a box of Scissors cigarettes to offer Bimalda. He took one cigarette and put it between his lips. I lit our cigarettes with a matchstick and began to think. His style of smoking is imprinted on my mind. It seemed as though he were trying to cover complicated footprints of worry with the smoke of the cigarette. He would constantly glance at his wrist-watch and if he caught me observing him, he would smile slightly. The meaning of those perfunctory smiles was not lost on me...

The three men who had accompanied him had fallen asleep in the car. Bimalda looked at his watch again and began to speak: 'How many children do you have?'

'A son and two daughters,' I replied.

'Do you like watching films?' he asked, standing up to take off his heavy overcoat and lay it on the back of this chair. Reaching for the box of cigarettes lying on the table, Bimalda took out the last one, put it to his lips and threw away the empty box.

'Shankarji,' he said, 'you have not yet told me whether you are interested in films or not...'

'Not too much,' I replied absently.

I took off my glasses and wiped them before wearing them again. Next I soldered the dry-connection of the machine, checked it with the meter, folded the sleeves of my shirt and turning to Bimalda, said: 'Sir, your work is complete now. You may call your men from the car and ask them to check it for themselves.'

Bimalda went out to the car and came back with his two assistants who checked each part of the machine.

'It is fine, dada, everything seems to be alright,' they said.

Bimalda turned to smile at me and said: 'Shankarji, now tell me, how much do we owe you?'

'Whatever you wish to give me Sir,' I replied.

Bimalda looked at his watch and said: 'Oh, it is nearly 4.00 am, but you have not said what you should be paid...'

'Make it thirteen hundred rupees,' I said.

He exclaimed, 'Surely that is too little!'

One of the men counted out the notes before handing them to me.

Holding the notes in my hand, I thought to myself: 'Thirteen hundred rupees for a single night, that is great!'

Perhaps he had caught the look of ecstasy on my face on receiving thirteen hundred rupees. Bimalda repeated: 'Shankarji, you have asked for very little money.'

He took out a thousand-rupee note from his wallet and said: 'Besides being a good mechanic, you are also a good man Shankarji.'

'Be that as it may Sir, I am not in the habit of being tipped!'

'This is not a tip; it is money that you have justly earned,' said Bimalda. 'Had we called a mechanic from Bombay or had I taken this part to Bombay—the cost would have been very high. In comparison to that expense, this is nothing.'

Holding the unexpected thousand-rupee note, I exclaimed, 'This is the richest night of my life!'

Bimalda's companions got into the car, while he stood by it and placed his hand on my shoulder, 'Shankarji, which day of the week do you close your shop?'

'Only on Sundays,' I replied.

'Very well! This Sunday, I will send the production car for you. Do come and watch the film-shooting. You can also see for yourself if the recorder is working properly or not!'

'Okay, Sir,' I replied, 'I am not very interested in the shooting, but yes, I would love to see Dilip Kumar in person.'

Bimalda was stepping into the car when he suddenly turned: 'Shankarji, I forgot my coat.'

I went inside and picked up the coat from the backrest of this very chair. I was astonished to find it so heavy! Even today, I can feel the weight of Bimalda's coat on my arm…

People gifted with sound cultural values generally live up to their word and keep promises. On the following Sunday, at the appointed time, the production car sent by Bimalda came to take us to Ranikhet. We were welcomed with great affection and warmth. Vyjayanthimala placed my son on her lap and played with him. The boy is a doctor today.

'The warm embers of that day have not died down till today. In the depth of my heart, that day never really ended. And the sparks of that rich night will always light up moments from the past…'

'*Aapke saath guzara hua lamha,*
Lutf lene baithoon, toh zindagi kam hai…'

(If I ruminate on those moments spent with you,
The pleasure can outlast a lifetime…)

Gyan Singh[2]

NOTES

[1]Original title: *Sabse mehngi raat* (Translated by Rinki Roy Bhattacharya with assistance from Preeti N. Singha).

[2]See list of contributors.

Madhumati's Place in Film History

Let me not to the marriage of true minds admit impediments…
—Shakespeare (*Sonnet 116*)

When Rinki invited me to join her mission to revisit the locations where *Madhumati* was shot and unravel the past, I jumped at the idea of an impromptu holiday of a different kind. Ranikhet was a place I had long wanted to see. But as the location (though vastly changed by the ravages of time) worked its magic, I was struck by how the iconic film had embedded itself into the collective memory of so many local people. Recollections filtered over time were amazing; and observing Rinki's excitement, I too was subtly drawn into the process of rediscovery. It is a privilege to see and then share a writer's excitement and engagement with a cherished project.

I have tried my best to distance myself from the immediacy—and may I say felicity—of this journey into the past, to explore *Madhumati*'s seminal place in our cinema with the objectivity of a critic. Forgive me if the enthusiasm of a participant peeps in at times.

But then, a journey undertaken without enthusiasm is futile…

A CLASSIC IS FOREVER

True—but there are classics *and* classics. A rare few are flawless masterpieces—defining an auteur for all time, surviving changing critical parameters and shifting film theory dicta with their deserved reputation intact. They are admired for their craft and pioneering place in film history. A few are also deeply loved over decades—an elusive accolade for many critically acclaimed films. Many more are cherished for other reasons, even when they don't fit into the master's oeuvre with seamless ease. *Madhumati* is Bimal Roy's most popular, commercially successful film. It is a landmark in its own way, a genre trendsetter, though it doesn't reach the poignant depth of *Devdas*, attain the stark, serene beauty of *Bandini*, pave the way for neo-realism as the path-breaking *Do Bigha Zamin* did, or rouse the conscience of casteist India with the endearing humanism of *Sujata*.

What then makes *Madhumati* so fondly loved over generations? The appeal of a love story that transcends death, accompanied by haunting music acting as an integral narrative track, in a land that staunchly believes in reincarnation is an obvious answer. Reincarnation was familiar to ancient Greeks but nowhere has the belief in the rebirth of the soul over many lives taken such deep root as in India—at the philosophical, religious, folk and everyday level. Allowing for metaphysical variations and interpretations, belief in reincarnation is integral to all Indic religions—Hinduism, Buddhism and Jainism as well as animistic faiths that have persisted in overt and covert forms at the symbolic level in rites of passage and rituals that mark them.

Madhumati is basically a love story which affirms the power of love over death, evoking subliminal associations—of faith and belief—that characterize the collective psyche of our society. A newly married couple is given the blessing that their union be for seven lives. Be it in poetic parlance or everyday idiom, 'Janam janmantar ka pyar' is a phrase that resonates with us both at an emotional and cultural levels. Actually, it is surprising that there are not that many memorable films centred on reincarnation, given our acceptance of the idea of rebirth. Could it be that over-familiarity with an idea reduced it to a cliché in lesser hands? It needs a leap of imagination and story-telling ability to raise a familiar cliché to the magical. And *Madhumati*'s enduring mystique spells magic.

Madhumati is the confluence of many geniuses—Bimal Roy, Ritwik Ghatak and Salil Chowdhury. Ghatak's story and script are unusual for a maverick visionary who sculpted an epic form of cinema out of the fusion of personal despair and tumultuous history that cleaved his beloved Bengal into two. Ghatak brings an unusual playfulness to his musically structured screenplay with an atmospherics-laden prologue, an operatic central love story and a life-affirming epilogue. It is a structure that has remained unique to *Madhumati*, though elements of the central mystery have provided inspiration, if not bequeathed a template, for later films of love, sudden death, rebirth and revenge formula.

Gothic mystery, first perfected in Kamal Amrohi's *Mahal* (1949), is an intriguing story that can't be reduced to an easy, comprehensible narrative graph. The components are striking: a haunted house teeming with palpable secrets, inscrutable portraits staring down almost balefully from walls supporting a vaulted ceiling, the sudden appearance and disappearance of a lovely young woman, a divinely beautiful Madhubala on a swing singing the alluring theme song and the final unravelling of a sinister plot that artfully invokes the supernatural to execute its fell purpose… And last but not the least, its B&W cinematography, revealing the influence of German expression brought into India cinema through the work of Franz Osten, magnifying the mystery.

Bimal Roy adapts the Gothic element of a shadowed mansion whispering its secrets and seamlessly marries it to the sunlit expanse of meadows and mists swirling over a rushing stream and filtering through the woods, to create a mood of lyrical tenderness alternating with menacing, pre-planned villainy. It is remarkable how much of *Madhumati* takes place outdoors; and when the action moves into Ugranarayan's mansion, the architectural elements—arches, long corridors ending at a barred exit, high ceilings with the chandelier swaying threateningly with intimations of impending doom—come into their own to heighten the sense of impending tragedy. The difference is that the tragedy of a love cruelly destroyed before culmination is poignant, and yet, it ends with the promise of redemption.

The prologue follows the classic path of building up curiosity and dread. A rainy night, a winding road, the classic gothic ploy of strangers arriving at a desolate ruin of a haveli, the massively forbidding door opening almost eerily without human intervention before we see the old retainer ushering in the travellers into its gloomy, cavernous hall. The silence is broken by unnerving sounds—a girl's voice, the heavy clanging of anklets, a girl's scream and heart-wrenching sobs. A portrait falls down from the wall and Deven recognizes his own brush strokes. His memories come back as the gauzy, frayed curtains envelope him…suggesting imprisonment as well as freeing of images from a past life. A collage of images follows: a girl's face behind a row of lilies, the gushing waves of a swift stream, the threat of hoof beats followed by a rider coming into the frame, culminating in the frontal view of a haveli in all its grandeur. Now we see Ugranarayan's face etched with hauteur and implacable purpose.

The prologue flows with the unstoppable rhythm of a mountain stream into the heart of the central love story. Deven recalls his past life as Anand, coming to the timber estate as its new manager. The mist parts to reveal the serene landscape in all its pristine beauty as he begins his joyous journey of anticipation to the strains of *Suhana safar aur ye mausam haseen*. But warnings of danger lurk everywhere. The song, full of carefree anticipation, ends as he reaches the edge of a cliff, and a woman's voice rings out a warning as the first strains of *Aaja re pardesi* waft over the wind. The opening lines are repeated, a slightly loner version now, when he is inside his quarters.

Masterly is the way silence and song are used to build up the strange mood. When Anand comes to the sign that says *Us paar jaana mana hai*—you wonder whether it is a warning or a beckoning to a forbidden Eden. *Us par jana mana hai*—a dire warning against the transgression of an invisible barrier; or a subterranean summons to explore what is beyond normal danger and discover the mystery of the past, the allure of the present and prescience of the future? *Aajare* is now a siren's song in all its alluring seduction and promise of fulfilment. We see Madhu standing on a rock from a distance, then gambolling through the stream. You see her clearly when the words *Bin tere har saans udasi* tease our imagination, tripping and running like a gazelle, playing a game of hide and seek amid magical mists and sylvan woods. Madhu's identification as a symbol of nature and innocence is complete with Anand's first sighting of her face, followed by a close-up of a flower in full bloom. A wood-nymph running wild—the epitome of a pure love waiting for her soulmate!

The songs flow into one another like an operetta; phrases and interludes echoed with precise deliberation to suggest a continuum of emotion. This continuum is not confined to the heart of Madhu and Anand's unfolding love. Madhu's trust and sense of waiting convey that this is a thread that has been picked up from a remembered past: *Tum sang janam janam ke phere, bhool gaye kyun sajan mere.* Could there be a more transparent articulation of a love that has transcended many lives, that this is simply another link in a chain of eternal love? The union is sanctified before the figure of a local deity when Anand anoints Madhu's maang with vermilion, claiming her as his wife in yet another life.

This evocation of the continuum of love is unique to *Madhumati* because none of the other films directly inspired by this theme—*Kudrat* (1981) and *Mehbooba* (1976), with big stars—can replicate this magical mood and mystique of undying love. Both *Mehbooba* and *Kudrat* starred Rajesh Khanna and Hema Malini, a commercially viable pairing. *Kudrat* had the angle of a psychiatrist probing a city girl's hallucinatory recalling of a life alien to her. The heroine is named Paro and Chandramukhi in her successive avatars. Can we read Chetan Anand's tribute to Bimal Roy's *Devdas* in it? Film history is full of such intended and unintended echoes of master works. Both in literature and film, Paro and Chandramukhi represent undying devotion; a devotion that dispenses with conventional decorum and its rigid rules!

Coming back to the heart of the story, the elaborate plan to unmask Ugranarayan's villainy borrows from *Hamlet*. Re-enactment of a crime follows *Hamlet*'s dictum: a play used as the tool to catch the conscience of a king. Ugranarayan is not exactly a king; but he represents the unholy marriage of feudalism and capitalism. Even a lyrical love story centred on reincarnation cannot be immune to the basic worldview of its maker. Bimal Roy and Ghatak manage to insinuate the socio-economic angle into a love story. By sensibility and ideological bent, both the director and his script writer were adherents of the IPTA School that espoused a leftist concern for the underprivileged. Ugranarayan is a feudal landlord turned exploitative businessman, like the landlord of *Do Bigha Zamin* who sells fertile agricultural land to the industrialist setting up a factory, thus causing the migration of uprooted peasants to city ghettos in search of livelihood.

Madhu's apparition is visible only to Anand after everyone—including her father—presumes that she has fallen prey to a wild animal in the jungle, not a rapacious man who lusted after her. Only Anand can hear her signature song and the heavy clang of her anklets. It is interesting that instead of the usual tinkling sound of anklet bells, Roy opts for a heavy, foreboding sound which alternates with silence, underlining its eeriness. After a despairing Anand finds a look-alike of Madhu in the sympathetic Madhavi and he sees her performing the Santhal dance, he plans to recreate the events of the fateful night. Johnny Walker's *Jungal me mor nacha* is a punctuation mark to demarcate a dramatic space between two significant events. The first is Anand's visit to Madhu's room on a stormy night when they make a formal vow of togetherness. Madhu says she will live with him and die with him. He counters, insisting on facing all storms so that she can sleep in peace. Their hitherto playful, tender banter—Anand teasing Madhu's naivete turns solemn, culminating in their marriage near the cave—an ancient deity and benevolent nature their witness. After the *Jangal mein mor nacha* comes the first climax, when Madhu is lured to the mansion on a stormy night after Anand has been sent away on an errand. The mansion is frontally presented, and a hound howls with its head raised.

The gothic comes into full play in the Hamletian unmasking of evil. A story night again, the howling of the hound indicating the torment of a soul's unfulfilled dreams, the chandelier swinging ominously, curtains flying in the wind, foot steps, clanking anklets, unbound hair and mesmerizing eyes willing you to follow her...with an enigmatic smile, Madhu calls out '*aao babuji*' while *Aajare pardesi* sounds for the last time. Anand falls to his death, summoned by his soulmate. The realization that it is not Madhavi but Madhu's apparition is a call to unite in death. Madhu's apparition is not ethereal; it echoes Hamlet's solid flesh lament. Initially, we assume it is Madhavi but the clue lies in the hypnotic gaze and mysterious smile. Vyjayanthimala has never had an ethereal presence. Roy trusts his camera to capture the intensity of her eyes and enigma of an unwavering smile to convey the supernatural.

The supernatural is often scary but *Madhumati* makes it a part of the romance, of the duality of love and death, the constant presence of one in the other. Madhu takes Anand to the cemetery of her ancestors and the gravestones are like sentinels marking time, a curiously comforting setting for the lovers. Madhu confesses to feeling at home here. Death is not to be feared but a recurring stage in an unending saga of meeting and parting. A promise of cleaving together in life and beyond!

The promise is fulfilled in the brief epilogue, when Deven welcomes Radha at the train station. Here too, there is the mild suspense of the train having met with an accident but Radha, his wife, survives the minor alarm. Their love finds fruition and affirmation in the little cherubic baby revealed to us.

Madhumati is a lyrical celebration of the erotic. The very first song *Suhana Safar* is pregnant with symbolism. *Woh aasman jhuk raha hai zameen par, yeh milan humne dekha yahin par,* evokes the primal symbolism of the union of *prakriti* and *purusha,* so central to Indian thought both spiritually and metaphorically. *Bichua* is an obviously erotic song that likens love's sting to a scorpion's bite, as true love drains out the poison. Though the dance itself is decorous, the lyrics are seeded with simple eroticism. *Madhumati* connects with *Do Bigha Zamin*'s opening song *Hariala sawan dhol bajata aya,* in its choreography. A line of dancers romp across the frame in a diagonal line and in *Madhumati,* you see this replicated in the line of local men and women going off to a fair while the musical prelude to *Zulmi sang aankh ladi* plays in the background. In the actual picturization of *Zulmi sang* the play between straight lines and circular formations suggests the dramatic chorus of IPTA plays. There is also an unexpected moment of grace while the camera pauses on a young girl dancing solo—an anonymous dancer given a few moments of screen time with such generosity.

In *Bichua* too, with its far more complex choreography as the camera intercuts the song with Anand's enthralled face, there is another remarkable juxtaposition of modesty and eroticism. The women encircle Madhu and raise their veils to form a canopy, shielding the love-stung maiden from prying eyes. An image of grace in movement!

Like all classic love stories, love transcends differences of class and society. Impediments to such a union only deepen commitment. *Madhumati*'s lovers embody the true marriage of minds and spirits. That is why the stress is on bringing Ugranarayan to justice and not seeking conventional vengeance! The unmistakable emphasis on justice is in harmony with Bimal Roy's sensibility. There is room for pain and suffering in his films, a hunger to set things right in an unjust world. But anger is alien to his culture, upbringing, sensitivity and worldview. There is enchanting serenity despite the tragic fate of the lovers in *Madhumati*—an elusive quality that fell short of films that followed its template.

Karz (1980) and *Karan Arjun* (1995) are some of the most successful films—in terms of box-office—using the reincarnation theme. In both cases, the driving force is revenge. Vengeance can be righteous; but most often it is impelled by violent anger and implacable hatred. Justice is a mere by-product. *Karz* is an adaptation of the Hollywood film *The Reincarnation of Peter Proud* (1975) and follows the thriller formula with not too much stress on the Indian concept of karma. *Karan Arjun* invokes the Mahabharat heroes and makes allies of arch rivals in their rebirth. The film is a celebration of male bonding and obedience to a vengeance-seeking mother. The love stories of the two protagonists are merely incidental.

Bees Saal Baad (1962) has often been spoken of as belonging to the *Madhumati*-genre. Except for the haunting song *Kahin deep jale kahin dil* and the implied presence of a ghost, the film is a loose adaptation of the Arthur Conan Doyle classic, *The Hound of Baskerville*. Just the recurrence of a haunting theme song and dependence on the supernatural does not make such derivatives true heirs of *Madhumati*. Actually, *Mahal's Aayega anewala* and *Madhumati's Aaja re pardesi* are kindred theme songs, redolent of love's eternal yearning.

The only other notable film that echoes the spirit of *Madhumati* is *Milan* (1967), starring Nutan and Sunil Dutt. *Sawan ka mahina pavan kare sor* is an evergreen song, energizing the melody with the vibrancy and playfulness of rustic enunciation. *Milan* is based on the Telugu film *Mooga Manasulu* (1963). The presence of a wide, expansive river is central to the love that burgeons between a rustic, worshipful boatman and the college-going daughter of a local landlord. Despite its melodramatic excesses, *Mooga Manasulu* (more than *Milan*) was limned with the authenticity of local idiom and charming use of dialect to underline love that survives class differences. Like *Madhumati*, in their next birth, the lovers are no longer separated by the class divide that looms so large in the central story.

Another recent success of this genre is the Telugu blockbuster *Magadheera* (2007), waiting for its Hindi adaptation (as befits the new Bollywood trend), directed by the phenomenally popular Rajamouli, starring Ram Charan Teja and Kajal Agarwal. The introduction to the reincarnated lovers takes up much screen time, following the usual path of boy meets girl, girl flounces away in disdain. That is until the hero, a stuntman, accidentally touches the girl and unfreezes locked memory that takes them to medieval Rajasthan from contemporary Hyderabad. *Magadheera* unleashes a fusillade of action and special effects, song and dance, to unravel the story of a warrior, a princess and a scheming commander-in-chief. Interestingly, the villain and his cohorts, along with the hero's helpful sidekick who also supplies the necessary comedy, are all reborn. Here, it is reincarnation en masse and the trick seems to have worked at the box office!

Om Shanti Om (2009) has the most obviously *Madhumati*-inspired climax. Farah Khan's film revels in paying tribute to

Bollywood while spoofing many of its standard clichés. The climax mirrors *Madhumati*, including the crashing chandelier and spirit appearing in place of the look-alike. And while Madhu and Anand fall to their death, in *Om Shanti Om*, it is fire that destroys both Shanti and the evidence. It is almost as if the theme has been finally cremated because it is impossible to replicate an inspirational classic.

                                                              Maithili Rao

Anklets Singing on the Breeze

The genre of the ghost story across cultures has been one to shape the integral belief systems of the community they arise from. *Madhumati* was born, allegedly from a challenge by then fledgling Bombay-based[1] director Bimal Roy to his then script writer and Bangla brother Ritwick Ghatak[2]. Whether this challenge—like a similar literary challenge that famously gave birth to one of the greatest stories of ghostly regeneration (*Frankenstein*)—was also placed on a dark and stormy night[3] is irrelevant. Two challenges held apart by time and culture; one in modern-day India spawning a haunting tale of reincarnated love and deception in *Madhumati* while the other is situated in Victorian England. Both relate to the emotional distress of loss and seeking identity in their day, and in their own peculiar way, shaped an entire generation. Two similarities emerge.

First, the fact that both stories were born of a challenge is notable. Mary Shelley's rising to the challenge of her then husband P.B. Shelley and their grand host Lord Byron, by creating overnight, the extraordinary tale of scientific experimentation playing at being god causes young and old readers and audiences across time to thrill with chilling fantastical horror.[4] *Frankenstein* still holds sway over the successful creation of fear at any mention of the name. The grotesque creation of one of the earliest prosthetic masks ever cast for an actor, still floats to mind the moment one hears the name.[5] In many ways *Madhumati* in an

Indian context has a similar effect on audiences familiar with the story. An Indian child dreads hearing the sound of phantom anklets in an isolated corridor. This fear may be traced ably to the girl ghost in *Madhumati*. Roy's successful rendition of a musical, yet terrifyingly silent, tinkle of the ghostly anklets as they sing and lilt across the breezes of hilly Nainital has marked the memories of an entire generation, even beyond, with an anticipated fear of hearing that sound on a dark night in a quiet corridor.

Then the second similarity—the Swiss villa where the challenge was set is not dissimilar in shape and form to the decrepit haveli where the dastardly Ugranarayan lays his plan to corrupt Madhumati. Speaking of dark and stormy nights marking beginnings, the opening of the film is marked by a dark lightning storm and a flickering candle. Beyond parallels however, these have endured as defining literary and film icons for an age.

When I first saw the film,[6] projected in silver and charcoal light on a fluttering sheet at Sophia College Bombay, that sound memory was what I came home with. It was impossible not to be terrified by the imaginary recurrence of that quiet jingle. Salil Chowdhury has also woven these bells most adeptly into the musical score of the film. The gentle, almost sad, tinkle of bells guiding the lifeless ankles of a lovelorn girl seeking her equally bereft lover. It seems to be the sound that connects them across the great chasm between the living and those beyond the veil. That lonesome jingling is the only sound that lilts and leads him, seeking to find a real source to the very real ringing in his ears, across the valley to where they used to meet. To the same spot, the shade between the trees where they first met, where they continued their forbidden tryst, and where their shadows play at noon when they no longer can. When Madhumati from the past flings herself, freeing herself, preserving her honour the only way our unfortunate women are taught we can,[7] by pelting down from the pinnacle of fear and plunging to her horrific end, it is that unpleasant silence after the relentless tinkling, jingle-jangle of those crazed bells on her running feet that the onlooker remembers. And that final, deathly silence!

The long, arduous efforts to retrace the making of *Madhumati* must be congratulated in itself. Then to have the story related: what a gift. A book of this sort, creating a tableau of anecdotal tales, recapturing lost voices before it is too late; the histories of the locations visited and shaped by the telling of this immortalized story is surely much-awaited by those who have grown up fearing hearing those anklets singing on the breeze.

Dr Anwesha Arya

NOTES

[1]Politically motivated name changes of geographical areas has long been an alienating tool of governance, currently being used across the subcontinent in some mistaken attempt to reclaim history. I use the name Bombay, as Bimal Roy would himself have referred to his then new home town.

[2]I don't believe it is possible to reliably corroborate the actual event; but in the family and among familiars it has come to be treated as part of our literary and film heritage as a truth rather than hearsay. May I therefore reiterate that here?

[3]Famously framed by the setting of Byron's Villa Dioati along the shores of Lake Geneva in Switzerland; for more anecdotal and historical references see: www.swissinfo.ch/eng/specials/extraordinary

[4]Fascinatingly the seeds for another great ghost/ horror story *Dracula* were sown that same night.

[5]Albeit, the name of the grotesque creature that Victor Frankenstein creates is never named. That is one of his pathetic pleas, his need to have a name and to find a friend, but the creature mistakenly has for posterity been dubbed the name of his genius, but doomed creator.

[6]Elsewhere, (See: Anwesha Arya [2008] 'Beyond Borders: Bimal Roy at Home and Abroad', 153-161 in, *Bimal Roy: The Man Who*

Spoke in Pictures edited Rinki Roy Bhattacharya). I noted how *Madhumati* came to be my most favourite of my grandfather's wonderfully rich movie-stories. It is for this reason I was invited to contribute my chapter.

[7]More on the gender implications of this violent aspect of the unfulfilled rape of a peasant girl by one of the landed gentry and the impossible legal ramifications that leave a community bereft in a forthcoming piece: *Madness in Madhumati: The Role of the Avenging Father in Indian Cinema.*

III

From the Archives

Credits

Story: Ritwick Ghatak

Dialogues: Rajinder Singh Bedi

Dialogue Director: S. Paul Mahendra

Director of Photography: Dilip Gupta

Associates: Apurba Bhattacharya, Chunilal Chatterji

Art Direction & Costume Design: Sudhendu Roy

Costume Designer for Vyjayanthimala: Yadugiri Devi

Settings: Manilal Somabhai

Editing: Hrishikesh Mukherjee

Associate: Das Dhaimade

Assistant Director: Moni Bhattacharjee

Audiography: Dinshaw Billimoria

Songs Recording: B.N. Sharma

Processing: Shamrao M. Dhurandhar

Choreography: Sohanlal, Satyanarayan, Sachin Shankar

Production Controller: Moni Bhattacharjee

Production Executive: M.D. Raman

Production Secretary: Madan Bakaya

Unit Managers: Sanjiva, Chandra and Pirachand

Publicity Executive: Amrit Shah
Stills: Kamat Foto Flash
Costumes: Kishen, Lakshmidas
Make-up: Jagatkumar and Bijoykumar

ASSISTANTS

Direction: Raghunath Jhalani, Debabrata Sengupta
Music: Kanu Roy
Photography: S. Mastan
Sound: Murar H. Patel
Editing: Sreedhar Misra
Make-up: Shanti
Production: Amrit, Basant, Rajkumar

Produced and Processed at: Mohan Studios
Recorded on: Gramophone Records:
R.C.A. Sound System   H.M.V.

Profiles of Madhumati Winners

Bimal Roy: Best Picture & Best Direction: Winning Filmfare Awards would seem to have become something of a habit with Bimal Roy, who has few rivals as a craftsman in the Indian film industry today. The fact that he has already won half a dozen trophies—two for Best Picture and four for Best Direction bears eloquent testimony to the quality of the pictures he has been making ever since he introduced the neo-realistic trend in our films with his *Do Bigha Zamin*. This bold venture secured for him the Filmfare Awards for Best Picture and Best Direction, and he repeated the achievement with his direction in *Parineeta* next year, performing a remarkable hat trick with *Biraj Bahu*. Equipped with an all-round knowledge of the mechanics of movie-making, Bimal Roy started his film career at New Theatres as an assistant cameraman to Nitin Bose. That was in the early 30s and he got his first big break in the late P.C. Barua's film *Devdas*, with which he emerged as a full-fledged photographer. He next turned his hand to film direction, affording glimpses of brilliance in his very first assignment, *Udayer Pathe*, made in Bengali. Making his bow on the all-India screen with *Hamrahi*, which was hailed as a classic, Bimal Roy followed it up with a number of films of outstanding merit like *Pahela Admi*, *Anjangarh* and *Maa*. The last venture gave him a firm standing in the film capital of India, and he soon set up his own production unit to give us one significant film after another. His latest award-winning film, *Madhumati*, has, unlike his other productions which did none too well at the box-office, enjoyed a good run all over India, and fully deserves the nine awards it has bagged, for it is a picture which can technically rank with the world's best.

Johnny Walker: Best Supporting Actor: Undoubtedly the top comedian of the Indian screen today, Johnny Walker twice narrowly missed winning the Filmfare Award, but his knack for repeating good performances has at last paid off and he earns the trophy for a diverting portrayal as Dilip Kumar's drunken side-kick in *Madhumati*. A revealing commentary on the tremendous popularity he has achieved is the fact that he is so far the only comedian to be cast in the hero's role in our films. His following among film fans is phenomenal and he has even had a film named after him. A very busy artist, he works almost round the clock, to fulfill his assignments in a dozen or more pictures at a time. So much success won in so short a time might easily have gone to anyone's head, but Johnny Walker remains as ebullient and friendly as he was when he tried his hand at a number of odd jobs, including that of a bus conductor, before entering films as an extra. And a 'bit' player he remained until Chetan Anand cast him in the role of a lame drunk in *Taxi Driver*. His work in that film brought him overnight popularity as a comedian, and since then, he has distinguished himself in a variety of roles. Among his more successful films are *Mr & Mrs 55*, *Pyaasa*, *Musafirkhana*, *Naya Daur* and *Aakhri Dao*. A performance of his deserving special mention is his role of the Marwari Seth in Ramesh Saigal's *Railway Platform*, for which he all but won the Best Supporting Actor Award. Johnny Walker is happily married to one-time film actress Noor and they have two children.

Salil Chowdhury: Best Music Director: A curious aspect of providing music in Indian films is that however popular a melody-maker's compositions may prove over the air, his name does not command marquee value until he works in a box-office hit!

This has been the experience of young and talented Salil Chowdhury, who made his debut in Hindi films five years ago as the music-director of Bimal Roy's *Do Bigha Zamin*. Since then, Salil has composed popular tunes in a host of pictures like *Naukri, Amanat, Jagte Raho, Tangewali, Musafir, Parivar, Ek Gaon Ki Kahani* and *Aawaz*. But it is only after his success in *Madhumati*, a picture which has done good business all over India that Salil Chowdhury has become a name that 'sells' in the industry. Perhaps the only music director in Bombay with a literary background, Salil began his movie career in Calcutta in 1931, and his music in the Bengali film, *Rangalaya*, earned him instant praise from critics and fans alike. Progressive in his ideas, Salil also wrote stories for the screen and, in 1954, he won the Best Story Award for *Rikshawala*. When Bimal Roy made a Hindi version of the film, he entrusted its music score to Salil, and the robust folk tunes of *Do Bigha Zamin* were widely appreciated. Salil continued the good work in his other assignments, but unfortunately for him, none of these films did well at the box-office. Though folk music was his forte—he is the founder of the Bombay Youth Choir—Salil adapted popular western tunes in his compositions with notable success, and took a bold step when he decided to introduce Dilip Kumar to the public in a singing capacity. Salil's first big break came with *Madhumati*, a chance he has seized with both hands to make his mark as a music-director in Hindi films.

Lata Mangeshkar: Best Playback Singer: To become something of a legend in one's lifetime is an honour given to few. Peerless Lata Mangeshkar can, therefore, be justly proud of the fact that hers is a name spoken with love and respect in every Indian home. She has won for the art of playback singing the honoured position it occupies in the film industry today. The high esteem in which she is held by music-lovers throughout the country is apparent from the fact that she has been voted the Best Playback Singer in the year of inception of this award. Truly, not one of her rivals commands the amazing range and versatility that characterize her singing, and she has certainly added to her stature by refusing to lend her voice to compositions likely to lower her standing as a singer with an enviable classical background. Born in a family noted for its musical traditions, Lata was fortunate to be groomed by her father, the late Dinanath Mangeshkar, a name celebrated in the field of Marathi classical music. Introduced by the late Ghulam Haider to films, she has sung under almost every music-director, having lent her voice in nearly a thousand films. Her capacity to render any song, be it an exposition of an involved classical raaga or a light composition, makes her the first choice of music-directors. *Jadoo, Andaz, Baiju Bawra, Shabab, Uran Khatola, Anarkali, Albela, Azaad, Barsaat, Aah, Chori Chori* and *Nagin* are some of her more successful films. The rare emotional depth that has marked her singing at all times is well reflected in the song *Aajare Pardesi* (from the film *Madhumati*) which has won her the award.

Shailendra: Best Lyricist: One of the most successful song-writers of the day is Shailendra, winner in its year of inception of the Filmfare Award for Best Lyricist for his composition *Yeh Mera Diwanapan Hai* in the film *Yahudi*. A man of radical views, Shailendra has happily refrained from introducing his progressive ideas into his songs, having, on the other hand, built up quite a reputation for himself as a master of the colloquial style. His compositions are noted for their smooth flow and easy cadence and, when set to music in their own inimitable style by Shanker and Jaikishen, come easily to the lips of music lovers. For over a decade, Shailendra took an active part in politics, at the same time attending 'Mushairas', where he made a name for himself as a poet. Introduced to films in 1948 by Raj Kapoor in his *Barsaat*,

Shailendra works with Hasrat Jaipuri when writing for Shanker and Jaikishen, but independently when teamed with other music directors like Salil Chowdhury and S.D. Burman.

Rajinder Singh Bedi: Best Dialogue Writer: A name well-known in contemporary Urdu literature, Rajinder Singh Bedi is among the most progressive and broadminded writers in the industry today. Born on 1 September 1915 at Lahore, Bedi has written and published several books, short stories, plays, and novels—which have been translated into various Indian and foreign languages. He has also worked with All India Radio in the capacity of a playwright and programme assistant, writing and producing plays over the air and was Station Director of Jammu and Kashmir Broadcasting Service. Feeling that his creative urge would find a better outlet in a progressive medium like films, Bedi began to write for the screen, and soon had an impressive roster of successful films to his credit. His pictures include *Bari Bahen, Bahu Beti, Do Sitare, Badnam, Naya Ghat, Daag, Barati, Mirza Ghalib* and *Milap*. Recently, he wrote the dialogues for *Devdas* and *Basant Bahar*. A few years ago Rajinder Singh Bedi launched into film production, his first film being *Garam Coat*, based on his own short story of that name. His concern's second venture was *Lal Batti*, and now their third production *Rangoli*, is on the floor. Rajinder Singh Beth wins the Filmfare Trophy for Best Dialogue Writer this year, the first time it is awarded, for his work in *Madhumati*.

Dilip Gupta: Best Cinematographer: If the panoramic beauty of India's countryside cast a spell on the cinegoer in *Madhumati*, the credit for achieving the effect should go to ace cameraman Dilip Gupta, who has been an important member of the Bimal Roy unit ever since the famous producer-director came to Bombay. Interested in painting and photography from childhood, Dilip Gupta started life as an actor in 1929 in Calcutta, playing an important role in *Chorkanta*, a silent picture produced by B.N. Sircar. His performance was so widely appreciated that the well-known producer offered him the leading role in his next venture, but the urge to make good in what was his first love, photography, triumphed and Gupta declined the offer. Instead, he took up an apprenticeship as an assistant cameraman to Nitin Bose, and, after working for two years at New Theatres, went to the USA and took a diploma in Cinematography from the New York Institute of Photography. He then joined Paramount Studios and received training under Virgil Miller, head of the Camera Section. He also utilized the opportunity to visit different studios in Hollywood and further enrich his knowledge of the art. On his return, many film-makers, including the late Himansu Rai, invited Gupta to join them, but he preferred to go back to New Theatres, where he worked for a number of years. He came to Bombay as a freelancer and has since photographed more than thirty films, with *Deedar*, *Naukri*, *Gotama The Buddha* and *Madh Bhare Nain* prominent among them. Dilip Gupta is regarded as one of the foremost cameramen in the country, but he modestly considers himself a student of photography.

Hrishikesh Mukherjee: Best Editor: Judicious editing was, until a few years ago, an art almost unknown to the makers of Indian films, for whom the function of the editor began and ended with the cutting and joining of scenes. To Hrishikesh Mukherjee, young, enthusiastic and imaginative, must belong, in a large measure, the credit of having won for this vital branch of movie-making its rightful place in the industry. Hrishikesh first afforded us a glimpse of his adroitness with the scissors in Bimal Roy's *Do Bigha Zamin*, having been spotted by the well-known producer-director in the New Theatres laboratory, where he worked for five years. A science graduate of Calcutta University, Hrishikesh was persuaded by Bimal to join the editing department, and the first film he edited was *Tathapi*. Since coming down to Bombay with Bimal Roy, Hrishikesh has, besides editing that producer's own pictures like *Naukri*, *Amanat*, *Devdas*, *Parivar* and *Apradhi Kaun*, displayed his skill in a number of other pictures like *Parineeta* and *Biraj Bahu*. The fact that he had travelled extensively all over Europe to study film technique was adequate qualification for Hrishikesh to turn his hand next to film direction, and his first picture, *Musafir*, though a poor draw at the box-office, was rated a classic by many who saw it. And now, with *Anari*, this enterprising craftsman has shown that he is quite capable of delivering the goods. Voted Best Editor for his work in *Madhumati*, Hrishikesh has won this award before for his work in Bimal Roy's *Naukri*.

Songs of Madhumati
(In Romanagari)

1.

Anand: *Suhana safar aur yeh mausam haseen*
Humein darr hai hum kho naa jaayen kaheen!

Yeh kaun hasta hai phoolon mein chhup karr?
Bahaar bechain hai kiski dhun parr?
Kaheen gungun, kaheen runjhun
Ki jaise naache zameen!
Suhana safar...

Yeh gori nadiyon ka chalna uchalkar
Ki jaise alhad chale pee se millkar
Pyare pyare, yeh nazaare, nikhaar hai
Harr kaheen!
Suhana safar...

Woh aasman jhuk raha hai zameen parr
Yeh milan humne dekha yahin parr
Meri duniya, mere sapne, milenge
Shayad yaheen!
Suhana safar...

Lyrics: Shailendra
Playback: Mukesh

2.

Madhumati: *Aaja re,*
Main toh kab se khadi is paar
Yeh akhiyan thak gayi panth nihaar
Aaja re, pardesi!

Main diye ki aisi baati
Jal na saki joh, bujh bhi na paati
Aa mil, mere jeevan saathi!

Tum sang janam janam ke phere
Bhool gaye kyun, sajan mere?
Tadpat hoon main saanjh savere!

Main nadiya phir bhi main pyaasi
Bhed yeh gehra, baat zarasi
Bin tere harr saans udaasi!

Lyrics: Shailendra
Playback: Lata Mangeshkar

3.

Girls: *Kancha le kanchi lai lajo*
Ghanti baje lalteen-wale lo!
Old man: *Naye naye raja toh naye taksaal*
Ho naye taksaal
Naye paise ko lekar aaya hai naya saal!
Girls: *Kancha le kanchi lai lagyo…*

Girl: *O more maali, ghar aaja*
Kal parson gin ginke
Balma beetey barson
Koi paati naa sandesa
Peeli padd gayi sarson
Girls: *Kancha le kanchi lai lagyo…*

Boys: *Rut matwali, jhoome daali daali,*
Jaane jag saara, jaane naa maali!
Girls: *Kali muskaye, bhaunre ko bulaye*
Jaane jag saara, jaane naa maali!

Girl: *Humre dil mein sau sau armaan*
Haaye, balam naa jaane
Girls: *Naa jaane, baalma, naa jaane!*
Girl: *Daal jhuki ambiyaan gadraai*
Koyal gaye gaane
Naa jaane, baalma, naa jaane!
Man more sajni, pyaar ki agni
Chorus: *Rut matwali, jhoome daali daali...*

Lyrics: Shailendra
Playback: Asha Bhonsle, Sabita Chowdhury, Ghulam Mohammad

4.

Girls: *Julmi sanng aankh ladi*
Julmi sanng aankh ladi, re!
Madhumati: *Sakhi main kaa se kahoon*
Ri sakhi kaa se kahoon
Jaane kaisi yeh gaanth padi
Julmi sanng aankh ladi, re!

Woh chhup-chhup ke bansuri bajaye
Sunaye mohe masti mein
Dooba hua raag, re
Mohe taaron ki chaaon mein bulaye
Churaye meri nindiya
Main reh jaaoon jaag re
Lage din chota, raat badi
Girls: *Julmi sanng aankh ladi, re!*
Julmi sanng aankh ladi...

Madhumati: *Baaton, baaton mein rog badha jaaye*
Humara jiya tadpe kisike liye shaam se
Mera pagal-pana toh koi dekho
Pukaroon mein chanda ko sajan ke naam se
Phiri mannpe jadoo ki chhadi
Girls: *Julmi sanng aankh ladi, re!*
Julmi sanng aankh ladi...

Lyrics: Shailendra
Playback: Lata Mangeshkar and Chorus

5.

Man: *Tan jale man jalta rahe*
Khoon-pasina dhalta rahe
Jeevan ka aara chalta rahe, Oho!
Group of men: *Tann jale...*

Man: *Oho, yeh hai zindagi, pyare*
Kaanton mein din guzaare
Phir bhi naa haare
Group of men: *Tann jale mann jalta rahe*
Khoon-pasina...

Group of women: *Chal ghar ko, sajan, mora nazuk badan*
Dekho main toh machal gayi, re
Main khadi dupariya mein jal gayi, re
Man: *Gori tujh ko sambhalna hoga*
Mere sanng sanng chalna hoga
Group of women: *Jaane kab takk jalna hoga*
Haaye-haaye, re
Group of men: *Tann jale mann jalta rahe*
Khoon-pasina...

Man: *Yeh toh hai zindagi, pyare*
Kaanton mein din guzaare
Phir bhi naa haare
Group of women: *Suno, saiyan, kahaani kati mann mein*
Jawaani lat suljhi, bikhar gayi, re
Umariya saari yunhi guzar gayi, re
Man: *Gori tujhko sambhalna hoga*
Mere sanng sanng chalna hoga
Group of women: *Jaane kab tak jalna hoga*
Haaye-haaye, re
Man: *Tan jale...*

Lyrics: Majrooh Sultanpuri
Playback: Dwijendra Mukherjee and Chorus

6.

Madhumati: *Ghadi-ghadi mora dil dhadke*
Haye dhadke, kyun dhadke
Aaj milan ki bela mein
Sarr se chunariya kyun sarke?

Saari umar ke badle, maine
Mangi thi yeh shaam
Aaj yaheen kho jaaoongi
Main unki bahen thaam, re
Pyar mila aanchal bhar ke
Dil dhadke! Kyun dhadke?
Aaj milan ki bela mein...

Aaj papihe tu chup rehna
Main bhi hoon chup-chap
Dil ki baat samajh lenge
Sanwariya apne aap, re
Dekh zara dheeraj dharke

Dil dhadke! Kyun dhadke?
Aaj milan ki bela mein
Sar se chunariya kyun sarke?
Ghadi-ghadi mora dil dhadke!

Lyrics: Shailendra
Playback: Lata Mangeshkar

7.

Anand: *Dil tadap-tadap ke keh raha hai aa bhi jaa*
Tu humse aankh naa chura
Tujhe kasam hai, aa bhi jaa!

Tu nahi toh yeh bahaar kya bahaar hai?
Gul nahi khile ke tera intezaar hai
Dil tadap-tadap ke...

Madhumati: *Dil dhadak-dhadak ke de raha hai yeh sada*
Tumhari ho chuki hoon main
Tumhare paas hoon sada

Tumse meri zindagi ka yeh singaar hai
Jee rahi hoon main ke mujhko tumse pyar hai

Anand: *Dil tadap-tadap ke...*
Madhumati: *Dil dhadak-dhadak ke...*

Anand: *Muskuraate pyar ka asar hai har kaheen*
Hum kahaan hain, dil kidhar hai
Kuch khabar nahi
Madhumati: *Muskuraate pyar ka asar hai har kaheen*
Hum kahaan hain, dil kidhar hai
Kuch khabar nahi

Both: *Kidhar hai kuch khabar nahi*

Anand: *Dil tadap-tadap ke...*
Madhumati: *Dil dhadak-dhadak ke...*

Lyrics: Shailendra
Playback: Mukesh and Lata Mangeshkar

8.

Madhumati: *O bichhua!*
Peepal chhaiyan, baithi palbhar
Bharke gagariya, haaye re
Chorus: *Haye re, haaye re, haaye re*

Madhumati: *O daiya re daiya re*
Chaddh gayo paapi bichhua
Female chorus: *O daiya re daiya re*
Chaddh gayo paapi bichhua
Madhumati: *O haaye haaye re marr gayi*
Koi utaro bichhua
Female chorus: *O haaye haaye re marr gayi*
Koi utaro bichhua
Male chorus: *Kaiso re paapi bichhua?*

Man: *O mantar pheroon, komal kaaya*
Chhodd ke jaa re—choon
Male chorus: *Jaa re! Jaa re! Jaa re!*

Madhumati: *O, aur bhi chaddh gayo*
Naa gayo paapi bichhua
Female chorus: *O aur bhi chaddh gayo*
Naa gayo paapi bichhua
Madhumati: *Kaisi aag laga gayo paapi bichhua*
Female chorus: *Kaisi aag laga gayo paapi bichhua*
Madhumati: *O saare badan pe chha gayo paapi bichhua*
Female chorus: *O saare badan pe chha gayo paapi bichhua*

Madhumati: *Mantar jhoota, vaid bhi jhoota*
Piya ghar aa re
Chorus: *Aa re! Aa re! Aa re!*

Madhumati: *Dekho re, dekho re, dekho utar gayo bichhua*
Female chorus: *Dekho re, dekho re, dekho utar gayo bichhua*
Man: *Toot ke reh gayo dannk, utar gayo bichhua*
Female chorus: *Toot ke reh gayo dannk, utar gayo bichhua*
Madhumati: *Saiyan ko dekh ke jaane kidhar gayo bichhua*
Female chorus: *Saiyan ko dekh ke jaane kidhar gayo bichhua*

Lyrics: Shailendra
Playback: Lata Mangeshkar, Manna Dey and Chorus

9.

Charan: *Jungal mein mor naacha, kisi ne naa dekha*
Haaye, hum joh thhodi si peeke zara jhoome
Haaye re, sab ne dekha

Gori ki gol-gol akhiyan sharabi
Karr chuki hain kaise kaison ki kharabi
Inka yeh zor-zulm kisi ne naa dekha
Hum joh thhodi si peeke zara jhoome
Haaye re, sab ne dekha

Kisi ko harre-harre note ka nasha hai
Kisi ko boot-suit-coat ka nasha hai
Arrey wah wah,
Yaaron, humein toh nau-taank ka nasha hai dekha
Hum joh thhodi si peeke zara jhoome
Haaye re, sab ne dekha
Jungal mein mor naacha, kisi ne naa dekha

Lyrics: Shailendra
Playback: Mohammad Rafi

10.

Anand: *Toote huye khwabon ne, hum ko yeh sikhaaya hai*
Dil ne jise paaya tha, aankhon ne gawaanya hai

Hum dhoondte hain unko, joh mil ke nahi milte
Roothe hain na-jaane kyun, mehmaan woh mere dil ke
Kya apni tammana thi, kya saamne aaya hai
Dil ne jise paaya tha, aankhon ne gawaaya hai

Laut aayi sada meri, takraa ke sitaron se
Ujdi huyi duniya ke sunsaan kinaron se
Par ab yeh tadapna bhi kuch kaam naa aaya hai
Dil ne jise paaya tha, aankhon ne gawaanya hai

Lyrics: Shailendra
Playback: Mohammad Rafi

Booklet Synopsis

The fruit of a deed is three-fold: it may arise here and now, or later, or in a succession (of lives)…

—Anguttara Nikaya

Receiving a telegram from his wife, Devendra hastily drives down to the station to receive her when a landslide due to heavy rains blocks the road forcing him and his doctor friend to take shelter, until the road is cleared, in an old, abandoned palace which was once owned by a succession of small Rajahs.

Inside, Devendra has a feeling that he has been there before. He talks of a picture on the wall and the old keeper affirms there was one…the doctor ascribes it all to the worried mind of Devendra. But no, a painting supposed to have been made by Devendra turns out to be exactly at the place where he had left it!

Images flit past. Yes, he came there once…as Anand, the manager of the timber-felling business on the estate of Rajah Ugranarayan. And, going out to sketch one day, he had come across a nimble-footed, sprightly Madhumati, the daughter of Pahan, the banished 'King' of the hill-folks.

Love between Anand and Madhumati grew as a sapling would tear-grow out of a cliff. Its branches and leaves had a typical wild growth, in nature's perfect setting until disturbed by the avaricious, lustful hands of Ugranarayan who sent Anand away on a flimsy errand. Once away, Bir Singh, a corrupt and vile employee of the Rajah reached Madhumati in the absence of her father to tell her that Anand had met with a serious accident and was calling her name, in the midst of his struggle between life and death, in the palace.

Madhumati, loving and unwary, rushed to the palace, only to find herself in the clutches of Ugranarayan.

Anand, back from his mission, went straight to Madhu's where Pahan was already premonishing Madhu's death, from burnt-out rice on the oven. Frantic search on the part of Anand and Pahan yielded no result. As Anand sank into hopelessness his elusive servant Charan appeared, only to inform that Madhu had been to the palace.

Anand rushes, enters the palace and challenges Ugra, whose men overwhelm Anand, beat him to pulp and throw him away from the borders of the estate. Gaining consciousness in a hospital, Anand's life became one constant vigil and as he prepared to go single-handed to have it out with the Rajah, there appeared a girl from the city, refined and sophisticated, every inch Anand's Madhumati.

And Anand got lost in the maze of Madhumati's, the trickeries of nature which had to yield to the biggest truth of life—Love!

The Filmindia¹ Review of Madhumati
(October 1958)

OUR REVIEW

Madhumati: A Handsome but Risky Experiment
Fine Technical Quality Fails To Save the Picture

There are certainly more things between heaven and earth than were dreamt of in the philosophy known to Horatio and one of them is the concept of reincarnation. Bimal Roy's *Madhumati* employs this concept, glorious and life-giving to many, to illustrate the eternal character of true and noble love.

The story contrived to put across this timeless theme, is unfortunately, both involved and trite. Besides bearing a discomforting resemblance to *Mahal Ashiana* (which in turn resembled Hollywood's *Portrait of Jennie*) and to the recent *Phagun*, *Madhumati* lacks the ethereal mood and the lyrical glow necessary to lend appeal and effectiveness to a picture abounding in supernatural events and carrying the stream of its narrative into the beyond. And the wind that blows in the story neither carries a perceptible scent of philosophy, nor does it succeed in transporting the spectator to that twilight region of existence where one is automatically inspired to discard reason as the key to the understanding of life and its numerous mysteries.

Instead of smoothly blending fact with fantasy, and suffusing the blend with the pristine emotion of love, the picture totters like an inebriate between earthly reality and other-worldly weirdness trying to fasten the two together with the sensation of melodrama. And though the picture proves to be short of breath and begins to pant early, it continues to be long in wind and footage providing the spectator many a dragging moment. In the result all its technical quality, which is excellent, fails to save the picture from being a pretty dull affair on the whole.

TALE OF TWO WOLVES

It all begins with Devendra, a grave-looking youth accompanied by a friend, racing in his car on a pouring wet night to the railway station to receive his wife. A dislodged boulder on the way, however, interrupts the journey and while the chauffeur goes to get help to remove the road-block, Devendra and his friend walk up to a deserted old mansion nearby for shelter. After being admitted inside by the keeper, Devendra begins to feel the eerie and empty mansion to be a familiar place although he had never visited it before. He points out some details about the house which prove his familiarity with it and after some further eerie business his memory begins to solve the mystery and the flashback starts.

Unrolling his previous life, the flashback shows Devendra as one Anand who arrives in a mountainous region to manage the rural office of a big estate-owner's timber business. Settling down in the place, Anand begins to supervise the felling of timber and unearth frauds in the previous accounts of the business. Alongside this, he visits the woods to draw sketches and to receive glimpses of a local belle who flits about amidst picturesque scenery jingling her anklets and sending flutters into his heart.

The belle happens to be Madhumati, the daughter of fierce-looking Pahan who was once upon a time the chief of hill-folks till he was once severely wronged by Bir Singh, a wily employee in the timber estate, and somehow deprived of his wealth and influence. Pahan and Madhumati now live all alone in a lonely house in the wild and mountainous region.

Anand and Madhumati, of course, attract each other with the force of gravity and their love goes on deepening despite Pahan making it plain that he did not want Anand, an employee of his enemies, to come near his house or his daughter. Once disappointed in a tryst, Anand pines so much to meet Madhumati that he enters her house ignoring her sleeping father. Roused from sleep, Pahan catches the lover and almost chops off his head but drops the axe upon being assured by him that he truly loves Madhumati and is prepared to marry her.

USUAL VILLAINY

Though approved of by Pahan, the romance between Anand and Madhumati now runs into a tougher obstacle which appears in the shape of Ugranarayan, the dissolute owner of the timber estate. Laying eyes on Madhumati, he is immediately struck with the desire to make her a morsel of his lust. Knowing her love for Anand and seeing no chance of having access to her charms peacefully, he lays an elaborate trap to outrage her. One night when Madhumati is left alone, with her father having gone away to attend a fair, Ugranarayan orders Anand also away on some flimsy business and then has word sent to Madhumati that Anand is lying in his mansion having been seriously injured in an accident. The news brings her running into the mansion where she finds only Ugranarayan and his animal passion. She struggles hard for her honour and saves it by jumping to her death from the roof of the house. The next day Pahan and Anand make a vain search for Madhumati till Anand, learning that Ugranarayan had called her to his mansion, goes to confront the rake. But the trouble brings Anand nothing except a severe beating. As Bir Singh proceeds to cast away the half-dead Anand, he is confronted by Pahan who settles the old score by killing Bir Singh and then collapsing into death himself.

Managing to reach a hospital, Anand gets well in due course and begins to move about in a dazed state.

And now coincidence shows Anand running into a picnic party, one of whom looks so alike Madhumati that he rushes after her screaming the name of his lost beloved. That brings him another manhandling, but somehow Madhumati's double, who calls herself Madhavi, shows sympathy for him and later she agrees to help him in getting Ugranarayan to confess his crime by visiting the villain on an appointed day in the dress of Madhumati.

A figure like Madhumati's does appear before Ugranarayan who takes her to be the ghost of his victim and in sheer fright blurts out the whole story of his crime leading to his arrest by the police. But Anand and the audience are amazed to discover that the ghost Ugranarayan had seen was not a fake one as per plan, as Madhavi who was to play that part arrives late on the scene. The experience provokes Anand into jumping to his death in the manner of Madhumati. The picture now returns to Devendra and his friend in the old, deserted mansion when Devendra's chauffeur appears to bring the good news that the road had been cleared and also the bad news that the train bringing Devendra's wife had met with an accident at the local station. Devendra rushes to the station to find his wife safe with their child crying behind in the compartment. And as one could well expect, Devendra's wife Radha looks exactly like Madhumati.

Most of the story takes place in the woods but one finds, besides the characters the author there too most of the time. And as presented, the story looks largely dull and pointless.

FIRST-RATE PRODUCTION

The production values of the picture are first-rate. The sets are good and convincing. The photography is a beautiful job. Dilip Gupta's camera catches some rarely picturesque outdoor scenery which would be more enjoyable but for the characters obstructing the view. The sound is well recorded. The dialogue is generally unremarkable. It is decidedly poor for a fantasy-flavoured theme. Some of the lyrics are tolerable. The music is good in places, a couple of songs being particularly pleasant. The direction of Bimal Roy is once again good in technical respects but ineffective in lending the necessary interest to the tale.

From the players, Dilip Kumar as Devendra and Anand is adequate without being particularly impressive. It would seem, however, that he does need better roles to keep his talent well-honed. Vyjayanthimala as Madhumati and as her various facsimiles doesn't have to do much beyond lending her looks and dancing talent to the roles which she does well without much obvious effort. Pran as Ugranarayan is effective as the villain. Jayant as Pahan fills the bill. Tiwari as Bir Singh looks wicked enough. From the rest Johnny Walker as a servant to Anand provides some usual comedy.

Madhumati is a picture of great pretensions but little merit. It is a good-looking, risky experiment.

NOTES

[1] 'Filmindia was a child of the New Jack Printing Press as Parker and Baburao Patel were good friends. Parker did not have much of an education but the plan to launch a magazine was as much his as his friend's. They had the press and paper was easily available because it was cheap in those days. B.B. Samant and Company could be depended upon to provide the advertising, not only for Prabhat-made movies but possibly others as well. All essential ingredients were in place. Baburao was a hard working and thoroughgoing man who did not believe in dreaming but hitting the nail on the head. It is a fact that with its very first issue, Filmindia started a new trend in Indian film journalism.' Quoted from Saadat Hasan Manto's book: *Stars from Another Sky: The Bombay Filmworld of the 1940s.* (Published by Penguin Books) Chapter: 'Baburao Patel: Soft-hearted iconoclast', pg. 183.

Before and After Madhumati
Filmography: The Feature Films of Bimal Roy

BEFORE MADHUMATI

FILMS IN KOLKATA

1944: *Udayer Pathe*

Producer: New Theatres

Story: Jyotirmoy Roy

Screenplay: Bimal Roy, Nirmal Dey

Cinematography: Bimal Roy

Editing: Haridas Mahalanabis

Audiography: Atul Chattopadhyay

Art Direction: Souren Sen

Music: Raichand Boral

Lyrics: Rabindranath Tagore, Sailen Roy

Choreography: M.K. Nayar

Actors: Radhamohan Bhattacharya, Debi Mukhopadhyay, Bishwanath Bhaduri, Jiben Bose, Tulsi Chakraborty, Puru Mullick, Boken Chattopadhyay, Binota Bose, Rekha Mitra, Meera Dutta, Leena Bose, Maya Bose, Smritirekha Biswas, Debabala, Rajlakshmi.

The Hindi version of *Udayer Pathe* was released in 1946 as *Hamrahi*. There were slight changes in the star cast but the technical crew remained the same.

This was probably the first time in our country when the film came before and the novel was published post release of the film. The film was a stupendous success at the box-office and the novel too became an unique bestseller. The novel was dedicated, quite obviously, to Bimal Roy.

1948: *Anjangadh*

Producer: New Theatres

Story: Subodh Ghosh

[The original Bengali short story is *Fossil*]

Screenplay: Bimal Roy

Cinematography: Kamal Bose

Editing: Haridas Mahalanabis

Audiography: Bani Dutta

Art Direction: Anil Bhattacharya, Sudhendu Roy

Music: Raichand Boral

Lyrics: Rabindranath Tagore, Jyotirindra Maitra, Sailen Roy

Actors: Raja Gangopadhyay, Bipin Gupta, Bhanu Bandyopadhyay, Manoranjan Bhattacharya, Indu Mukhopadhyay, Tulsi Chakraborty, Jiben Bose, Bhaskar Deb, Boleen Som, Purnendu Mukhopadhyay, Jahar Roy, Sadhan Sarkar, Prafulla Mukhopadhyay, Sunanda Devi, Amita Bose, Parul Kar, Chhobi Roy, Manorama Devi.

The Hindi version of *Anjangadh* was also released in 1948. There were slight changes in the star cast but the technical crew remained the same.

1949: *Mantramugdha*

Producer: New Theatres

Story: Banaphool

[*Mantramugdha* is a play in Bengali]

Screenplay: Bimal Roy, Sudhish Ghatak

Cinematography: Kamal Bose

Editing: Subodh Roy

Audiography: Loken Bose

Art Direction: Sudhendu Roy

Music: Raichand Boral

Lyrics: Rabindranath Tagore, Banaphool

Actors: Jiben Bose, Sunil Dasgupta, Shakti Bhaduri, Kalipada Sarkar, Tulsi Chakraborty, Indu Mukhopadhyay, Jahar Roy, Bhanu Bandyopadhyay, Meera Sarkar, Reba Devi, Manorama Devi, Roma Nehru, Leelavati, Shefali Sarkar, Parul Kar.

1950: *Pahela Admi* (Hindi)

Producer: New Theatres

Story: Nasir Hussain (Ex INA),

Screenplay: Bimal Roy

Dialogues: Nasir Hussain, Pandit Bhushan

Additional Dialogues: Bidhayak Bhattacharya

Cinematography: Kamal Bose

Editing: Haridas Mahalanabis

Art Direction: Sudhendu Roy

Set Decoration: Sunity Mitra

Audiography: Loken Bose

Music: Raichand Boral

Lyrics: Flt Lt Prakash [Ex INA]

Choreography: Balkrishna Menon

Actors: Smriti Biswas, Ashita Bose, Balraj Vij, Vijoy Kumar [Ex INA], Pahary Sanyal, Paul Mahendra, Hiralal [Ex INA], Asit Sen, Bhupendra Kapoor, Jahar Roy, Prem Charan [Ex INA], K. C. Sharma, Bela Bose, Sreemati, Pravat Kumar, Robins, Major Puran Singh [Ex INA], Flt Lt Prakash [Ex INA], Capt. Nand Singh [Ex INA].

FILMS IN BOMBAY

1952: *Maa*

Producer: Ashok Kumar and Savak Vacha (The Bombay Talkies Limited)

Story: Swaraj Banerji

Scenario: Bimal Roy

Dialogues: Navendu Ghosh

Cinematography: Joseph Wirsching

Editing: Hrikishikesh Mukherjee

Audiography: J.M. Barot

Art Direction: D.N. Jadhav

Music: S.K. Pal

Lyrics: Bharat Vyas

Actors: Leela Chitnis, Bharat Bhushan, Shyama, Nazir Hussain, Kumud, Paul Mahendra, Manju, B.M. Vyas, Kusum Deshpande, Achla Sachdev.

1953: *Do Bigha Zamin*

Producer: Bimal Roy Productions

Story: Salil Chowdhury

Scenario: Hrishikesh Mukherjee

Hindi Dialogues & Dialogues Direction: Paul Mahendra

Cinematography: Kamal Bose

Editing: Hrishikesh Mukherjee

Audiography: Essa M. Suratwala

Art Direction: Gonesh Basak

Music: Salil Chowdhury

Lyrics: Shailendra

Choreography: Prem Dhawan

Actors: Balraj Sahni, Nirupa Roy, Ratan Kumar, Murad, Rajlakshmi, Nana Palsikar, Noorjahan, Nazir Hussain, Rekha Misra, Chitra, Jagdip,Tiwari, Sarita Devi and Meena Kumari (in a guest appearance).

1953: *Parineeta*

Producer: Ashok Kumar Productions

Story: Sarat Chandra Chattopadhyay

Scenario: Bimal Roy

Additional Dialogues: Nabendu Ghosh

Hindi Dialogues: Vrajendra Gaur

Cinematography: Kamal Bose

Editing: Hrishikesh Mukherjee

Audiography: Sherali Pabani & J.M. Barot

Art Direction: Jadhav Rao

Music: Arun Kumar Mukharji

Lyrics: Pt Bharat Vyas

Choreography: Gopi Kisan

Stage Dance: Gopi Kisan and Roshan

Actors: Ashok Kumar, Meena Kumari, Ashit Baran, Baby Sheela, Nazir Hussain, Badri Prasad, Pratima Devi, Rekha, Manju, Manorama, S. Bannerji, Nayana, Sarita, Bhupen Kapoor, Vikram Kapoor, Sailen Bose, Shivajibhai, Omprakash, Colin Pal, Baby Rehana, Baby Mumtaz & Tiwari (Guest Artiste)

1954: *Naukri*

Producer: Bimal Roy Productions

Story: Subodh Basu

Screenplay: Nabendu Ghosh

Hindi Dialogues: Paul Mahendra

Cinematography: Kamal Bose

Editing: Hrishikesh Mukherjee

Audiography: Dinshaw Billimoria

Art Direction: Sudhendu Roy

Music: Salil Chowdhury

Lyrics: Shailendra

Actors: Kishore Kumar, Sheila Ramani, Kanhaiyalal, Noor, Achala Sachdeo, Bikram Kapoor, Krishnakant, Tulsi Chakravarty, Bhupen Kapoor, Sunil Das Gupta, Iftekar, Jagdip, W.M. Khan, Samson, Moni Chatterji, Sheojibhai, Sailen Bose, Mahmud, Dubey, Girdharilal, Shakuntala Devi, Collin Pal.

1954: *Biraj Bahu*

Producer: Hiten Chaudhury
Story: Sarat Chandra Chattopadhyay
Scenario: Bimal Roy
Screen Adaptation: Nabendu Ghosh
Hindi Dialogues: Nasir Hussain
Cinematography: Dilip Gupta
Editing: Hrishikesh Mukherjee
Audiography: Essa M. Suratwala
Art Direction: Sudhendu Roy
Music: Salil Chowdhury
Lyrics: Prem Dhawan
Actors: Kamini Kaushal, Abhi Bhattacharjee, Shakuntala, Pran, Randhir, Manorama, Kammo, Bikram Kapoor, Iftekar.

1954: *Baap-Beti*

Producer: S.H. Munshi
(Story inspired by Guy de Maupassant's *Simon's Papa*)
Adaptation: Nabendu Ghosh
Scenario: Bimal Roy
Dialogue Translation: Mohanlal Bajpai
Cinematography: Kamal Bose
Editing: Hrishikesh Mukherjee
Audiography: B.M. Saha
Art Direction: Gurjit Singh
Music: Roshan

Lyrics: Pradeep

Choreography: L.C. Mathur

Actors: Ranjan, Baby Tabassum, Sunalini Devi, Nazir Hussain, Nana Palsikar, Baby Naaz, Sabita, Nalini, Anju, Kanta Kumari, C.L. Shah, Krishnakant, Anwaribai, Dolly, Mridula.

1955: *Devdas*

Producer: Bimal Roy Productions

Story: Sarat Chandra Chattopadhyay

Screenplay: Nabendu Ghosh

Hindi Scenario: Rajinder Singh Bedi

Cinematography: Kamal Bose

Editing: Hrishikesh Mukherjee

Audiography: Essa M. Suratwala

Art Direction: Sudhendu Roy

Music: S.D. Burman

Lyrics: Sahir Ludhianvi

Choreography: Hiralal

Actors: Dilip Kumar, Vyjayanthimala, Motilal, Suchitra Sen, Nazir Hussain, Murad, Kanhaiyalal, Moni Chatterjee, Iftekar, Nana Palsikar, Baby Naaz, Pratima Devi, Kammo, Sarita Devi, Shakuntala. Pran and Johny Walker (As Guest Artistes).

1958: *Madhumati*

Producer: Bimal Roy Productions

Story: Ritwick Ghatak

Dialogues: Rajinder Singh Bedi

Dialogue Direction: S. Paul Mahendra

Cinematography: Dilip Gupta

Editing: Hrishikesh Mukherjee

Associate: Das Dhaimade

Audiography: Dinshaw M. Billimoria

Art Direction: Sudhendu Roy

Music: Salil Chowdhury

Lyrics: Shailendra

Choreography: Sohanlal, Satyanarayan, Sachin Shankar

Actors: Dilip Kumar, Vyjayanthimala, Johny Walker, Pran, Jayant, Tiwari, Misra, Sheojibhai, Tarun Bose.

AFTER MADHUMATI

1958: *Yahudi*

Producer: Savak B. Vacha

Screenplay: Nabendu Ghosh

Associate Screenplay: R.K. Soral

Dialogues: Vajahat Mirza

Cinematography: Dilip Gupta

Editing: Hrishikesh Mukherjee

Audiography: Dinshaw M. Billimoria

Art Direction & Costume Design: Sudhendu Roy

Music: Shankar-Jaikishan

Lyrics: Shailendra, Hasrat Jaipuri

Choreography: Suryakumar, Vinod Chopra, Satyanarayan

Actors: Sohrab Modi, Dilip Kumar, Meena Kumari, Nigar Sultana, Nazir Hussain, Anwar Hussain, Minu Mumtaz, Murad, Bikram Kapoor, Baby Naaz, Helen, Cuckoo, Kamala Laxman.

1959: *Sujata*

Producer: Bimal Roy Productions

Story: Subodh Ghosh

Dialogues: Shailendra

Dialogue Direction: Paul Mahendra

Cinematography: Kamal Bose, Montu Bose

Editing: Amit Bose

Audiography: Essa M. Suratwala

Art Direction: Sudhendu Roy

Music: S.D. Burman

Lyrics: Majrooh Sultanpuri

Choreography: Satyanarayan

Manipuri Dance: Little Ballet Troupe

Actors: Nutan, Sunil Dutt, Shashikala, Lalita Pawar, Tarun Bose, Sulochana, Asit Sen, Ashim Kumar, Paul Mahendra, Baij Sharma, Brahm Dutt, Moni Chatterjee, Sabitri, Sheojibhai, Master Sohni, Baby Farida, Baby Shobha.

1960: *Parakh*

Producer: Bimal Roy Productions

Story: Salil Chowdhury

Dialogues: Shailendra

Dialogue Direction: Paul Mahendra

Cinematography: Kamal Bose

Editing: Amit Bose

Audiography: George D'Cruz

Art Direction: Sudhendu Roy

Music: Salil Chowdhury

Lyrics: Shailendra

Choreography: Badriprasad

Actors: Sadhana Shivdasani, Durga Khote, Leela Chitnis, Sheela Rao, Ruby Paul, Mumtaz Begum, Sarita Devi, Meherbanoo, Nishi, Vasant Chowdhury, Nazir Hussain, Kanhaialal, Jayant, Rashid Khan, Asit Sen, Paul Mahendra, Motilal.

1962: *Prem Patra*

Producer: Bimal Roy Productions

Story: Nitai Bhattacharya

[This was adapted from the super-hit Bengali film *Sagarika* (1956), starring the golden pair of Bengali cinema, Uttam Kumar & Suchitra Sen]

Screenplay: Salil Chowdhury, Debobrata Sen Gupta

Dialogues: Rajinder Kishan

Cinematography: Dilip Gupta

Editing: Amit Bose

Audiography: M.R. Pitle

Art Direction: Sudhendu Roy

Music: Salil Chowdhury

Lyrics: Rajinder Kishan, Gulzar

Actors: Sadhana, Shashi Kapoor, Seema, Rajendra Nath, Sudhir, Chand Usmani, Parveen Chowdhury, Padma Devi, Bela Bose, Sarita Devi.

1963: *Bandini*

Producer: Bimal Roy Productions

Story: Jarasandha

(The original Bengali novel is *Tamoshee*)

Screenplay: Nabendu Ghosh

Dialogues: Paul Mahendra

Cinematography: Kamal Bose

Editing: Madhu Prabhavalkar

Audiography: Dinshaw Billimoria

Art Direction: Sudhendu Roy

Music: S.D. Burman

Lyrics: Shailendra, Gulzar

Actors: Ashok Kumar, Nutan, Dharmendra, Raja Paranjape, Tarun Bose, Asit Sen, Chandrima Bhaduri, Moni Chatterjee.

DOCUMENTARIES OF BIMAL ROY

1943 *Bengal Famine*

1961 *Immortal Stupa*

1963 *Life and Message of Swami Vivekananda*

1967 *Gautama the Buddha*

Filmography compiled by: Sounak Chacraverti. With inputs by Rinki Roy Bhattacharya and SMM Ausaja

Afterword

Madhumati, the film that still haunts us!

The late Bimal Roy was my mother's uncle. He passed away when I was very young—unable to retain any vivid memories of him. Yet it seems that I knew my grand-uncle closely, as my mother would often tell me stories about her favourite uncle Monikaku when I was a child. The first of her generation, my mother was naturally the centre of everyone's affection, especially her doting uncle, till the next child of the family came along— the author of this book, Rinki mashi.

Godiwala Bungalow, or Number 5, Mount Mary Road, Bandra in Bombay where Bimal Roy spent most of his working life was like a second home (my second mama bari). Entering the huge drawing room of this grand Parsi bungalow, the first thing one noticed was a life-size portrait of an imposing man, towering over a neat row of female statuettes. It was not until many years later that I realized these were the famous Filmfare Trophies and the man in the portrait was Bimal Roy—the recipient of the highest number of these awards, until recently.

I remember an occasion when the family decided to screen *Madhumati* at a relative's home, hiring a 16mm projector, on his birth anniversary. I was in junior school at the time and can still recall the eerie impression that the film left on me. I am not in the least qualified to comment on the position that Bimal Roy commands in the history of Indian film-making; neither do I have the audacity to evaluate any of his films, let alone *Madhumati*. Yet, this particular film raises a few curious issues in my mind.

In the entire body of Bimal Roy's work, this film stands out as the odd one, different from the rest. In the beginning of his professional life, the subjects of his films like *Udayer Pathey* or *Do Bigha Zamin* reflect his socialist mindset bearing testimony to his association with the IPTA. His later films, mostly adapted from eminent Bengali writers, raised relevant social issues of the time and conceived with mature and aesthetic sensibility, his films were always meticulously crafted. Human relationships were given sensitive treatment in his works, steeped in realism. *Madhumati* comes as a break in the continuity one finds in his work of a realistic genre. In its structure and treatment, *Madhumati* bears the distinct Bimal Roy stamp—evocative imagery, simplicity of narration, handling dramatic sequences with restraint and brilliant imaging of haunting melodies.

Madhumati continues to puzzle me. It makes me wonder if Bimal Roy simply wanted to break away from his realistic tradition with a supernatural subject. Was this just to experiment with a different genre? Or did he leave his comfort zone to test if he could succeed in unchartered territories? *Madhumati* was after all one of the biggest box office successes in the history of Indian cinema.

I have heard Bimal Roy admired Hitchcock films. In certain sequences of his films, one detects a Hitchcockian touch. Had he not died young, I am convinced he would have experimented with varied styles and genres, as he did with such immense success in *Madhumati*.

Madhumati's credit titles roll like the who's who of Indian cinema: music—Salil Chowdhury; lyrics—Shailendra; editing—Hrishikesh Mukherjee; art direction—Sudhendu Roy; dialogues—Rajinder Singh Bedi; screenplay—Nabendu Ghosh;

cinematography—Dilip Gupta and lastly, the big surprise, story—Ritwick Kumar Ghatak...a legend in his own right. Add to this formidable list, the captain of the ship, Bimal Roy. A glittering galaxy of icons combined to create this amazing piece of cinema that still continues to haunt us.

But why did Rinki mashi chose me of all people to write an afterword for her book on *Madhumati?* Could it have something to do with the spooky connect?

I wonder...

Anik Dutta

Acknowledgements

This book of memories would not exist, but for the magic of Indian cinema, now in its centenary year. I was fortunate to have lived within that world of magic. And now to the credits that are due in the creation of this book...

Firstly for Baba—without his tireless, sleep-deprived and smoke-filled nights, none of us would have known the gem *Madhumati*, a celluloid history today. As I cannot express my gratitude in person, this book is in memoriam. This absorbing and extraordinary ghost story would not have been possible without the genius that was Ritwick Ghatak. I offer my profound respect to these irreplaceable men of magic in the form of this book of memories, writing it was like a pilgrimage in search of my missing father.

Secondly, to the cast of creators involved in this book. I am grateful to Anik Dutta; his epilogue sets an appropriate tone of nostalgia for a trip down memory lane. Both Maithili Rao and Anwesha Arya lent valuable observations, strengthening the creative process of re-creating the past. Sounak Chacraverti's compilation of a comprehensive filmography of my father Bimal Roy sets the necessary bolts in place to hold down so much more.

It all began with a need to retrace Baba's footsteps to Kumaon; to visit and imagine what he must have seen and felt before he set about to create. People appeared from previously unknown quarters, with anecdotes, advice and most importantly, a cup of chai. Deep and Hanshi Bhatt deserve special thanks for accompanying me on the Kumaon trip. Indeed it was Deep who unearthed the extraordinary episode at Shankar Radio and discovered Gyan Singh. I thank Dr Mala Srikanth for finding places and people connected with the making of *Madhumati* in Kumaon. And Professor Rajshekhar Pant for sharing his personal reminiscences of the outdoor location of *Madhumati* in Bhowali and Gethia.

A happy coincidence led me to fertility expert Dr Razia Husain from Aligarh. Her fortuitous meeting with Dilip Kumar, an actor we mutually adore, was an important breakthrough in the rebuilding of the *Madhumati*-Kumaon connection. Razia is the sole eyewitness to the creation of the magic we know today as *Madhumati*. To add to our good fortune, both Razia and Professor Pant substantiated those magical moments with photographs that lend the book its rich archival flavour.

Debabrata Sen, my father's first AD, deserves my high regard. Debu's eyes and his personal nuggets went a long way towards reliving that sepia-tinted period. Working on the book, I was forced to quiz him at odd hours and always found him willing, in spite of chronic health problems. His frequent interjections of: '*Amar mone nei*' (I do not remember!), gave me heart attacks till I was revived with yet another telling anecdote.

Among other notable contributors and people that I am deeply thankful to: freelancer Taran Khan who features in my opening chapter and the obliging Mr Joshi our helpful Bhowali guide. Special thanks are due to the National Film Archive for sourcing archival material.

My publishers Rupa Publications, India, have been especially supportive; in particular Elina Mazumdar and Ritu Vajpeyi-Mohan. A much-needed advantage that all writers appreciate, to have an understanding publisher and editor! Crucially, Mita Kapoor, my agent brings daily insight into the complex world of book trading and publicity that I could not have fathomed alone. Thanks are due to these extraordinary women.

A quick word of gratitude to the Datakino archives for opening the doors to the treasure trove and lending me some B&W stills of *Madhumati*.

And finally, I am thankful for the spontaneous support this book received from the three lead stars of *Madhumati*. At ninety, Pran Sahab's memory was fragile; but thanks to the personal interest of his daughter Pinky Bhalla—a compilation of this superlative actor's memories was possible.

Ms Saira Banu was helpful in chronicling the *Madhumati* chapter from Dilip Kumar's mental note book. I am truly grateful to the iconic screen couple for their time and patience. Vyjayanthiji's encouragement brought courage and hope when I needed it most. Indeed, her evocative Foreword laced the book with true authenticity.

The additional bonus of having a few words on my father from the movie icon Amitabh Bachchan stamps this book with contemporary relevance.

List of Contributors

Anik Dutta

Anik is a well-known copywriter based in Kolkata. He has written and made several corporate films. His maiden fiction film *Bhooter Bhobishyot*, a landmark in innovative cinema, was declared a super hit running non-stop for 150 days. His second film *Ashcharjo Pradeep* has been favourably reviewed. Anik is Bengal's new age film-maker.

Dr Anwesha Arya

Anwesha Arya teaches Cinema as an Instrument of Social Change—the Human Rights and Gender Perspective. With her background as a historian and anthropologist, she has fifteen years experience in research and film-making in the fields of gender, human rights and women's empowerment.

Bunny Reuben

Bunny Reuben, a close associate of Raj Kapoor, was a noted Public Relations man in the 1950s in the film-industry. The films he produced include *Anari* (1959) starring Raj Kapoor and Nutan and *Aashiq* (1962) starring Raj Kapoor and Padmini. Reuben authored a book on Dilip Kumar titled: *Dilip Kumar, Star Legend of Indian Cinema: The Definitive Biography* (Harper Collins)

Dr Clare Wilkinson-Weber

Clare M. Wilkinson-Weber teaches anthropology at Washington State University, Vancouver. Her 1999 book *Embroidering Lives: Women's Work and Skill in the Lucknow Embroidery Industry* was published by SUNY Press. Since 2002 she has been researching the Mumbai film industry, and has published several articles on her work. Her book, *Fashioning Bollywood: The Making and Meaning of Hindi Film Costume* was published in 2013.

Debabrata Sengupta

Debabrata Sengupta joined Bimal Roy as an Assistant Director with *Yahudi* (1956). Along with Raghunath Jhalani, he assisted Bimal Roy for most of his films until the film-maker's demise. Sengupta directed the Indian version of Shakespeare's *Comedy of Errors*: titled *Do Dooni Char* (1968), starring Kishore Kumar, Tanuja and others.

Gyan Singh

Gyan Singh was born into a middle-class family of Kaankar Tolla, a small locality of the old city of Bareilly. The family shifted to Amritsar before partition. He is fond of reading, writing, painting and films but did not have the opportunity to receive formal education. He worked at Sun Centre, Mumbai, as a film designer. Currently he spends time writing stories and songs and painting.

Maithili Rao

Rao, a leading film critic contributes to the London-based *South Asian Cinema*, *Man's World* and *Frontline*, continuing a decade-long association with *The Hindu* group, having been a regular contributor to the *Sunday Magazine* section of *Hindu*.

Raj Shekhar Pant

Raj Shekhar Pant is Head of Department, English, in Birla Vidyamandir—a heritage school commissioned in the nineteenth century. It had housed Oak Openings (where Jim Corbett is believed to have done his primary education), Philander Smith College, and finally one of the three Hallet War Schools opened during the World War II. He has also published over a thousand articles, interviews, reports and features with photographs in almost all the leading papers and magazines of India.

Dr Razia Husain

Dr Husain is the second lady doctor from Rampur State. She joined UP medical services as a gynecologist and was later posted to various districts of UP. Her father, Mr Abdul Jabbar Khan, was the chief civil engineer for the Nawab of Rampur whose summer resort in Ghorakhal Estate was where a major part of the *Madhumati* outdoor took place in 1957. An ardent fan of Dilip Kumar, she named one of her daughters Tarana, after the film starring Dilip Kumar and Madhubala. Incidentally, her son is named Saleem after Dilip Kumar's character in *Mughal-e-Azam*!

Sounak Chacravarti

Sounak completed his Masters in Comparative Literature from Jadavpur University in 1998. He is active in the field of publishing and art since 1999. His first publication, a collection of essays on the acclaimed Bengali poet Shakti Chattopadhyay (1934–1995), is considered an important critical work. Sounak co-edited the book *Prasanga: Shakti Chattopadhyay* with the famous writer and poet Sunil Gangopadhyay (1934–2012).